T0283629

"I read a lot of books about science and nature, yet rarely do I find a book that feels so welcoming and accessible while also delivering important and novel information; I wrote in the margins on each page exclamations of wonder and awe, and I learned many new concepts about forest ecology. Tapper takes a wide view back into the history of human disturbance in nature, and a philosophical overview of how we can work toward a more mutualistic relationship with the forests in the future. This is a manifesto against apathy, for as Tapper came to realize in his early days as a forester, there's 'nothing radical about doing nothing.' Tapper offers insights and suggestions for how to love a forest sustainably."

—Frances Cannon, interdisciplinary writer, editor, educator, and artist; Mellon Science and Nature Writing Fellow at Kenyon College

"Forests are a place so many of us find peace, inspiration, and balance, yet the complexity of our relationships with these ecosystems and the reciprocal role we play as stewards is seldom acknowledged. *How to Love a Forest* bravely and eloquently explores the powerful connections made and restored by engaging fully with the ecology, wonders, and challenges found in our forests, providing an important perspective of love, care, and action so needed at a time of unprecedented change."

—Tony D'Amato, professor of Silviculture and Applied
Forest Ecology, and Forestry Program director,
Rubenstein School of Environment and
Natural Resources, University of Vermont

"How do we fix a broken world? With patience and love, Ethan Tapper reveals the hidden historical forces that have sculpted our landscapes, and proves that, given enough wisdom and labor, we can still restore our degraded forests. If Aldo Leopold were a twenty-first-century Vermont forester with one good eye and a contemporary understanding of power and privilege, this might be the sort of book he'd write."

—Ben Goldfarb, author of *Eager: The Surprising, Secret
Life of Beavers and Why They Matter* and *Crossings:
How Road Ecology Is Shaping the Future of Our Planet*

"This is an unforgettable story from an important new voice in nature writing. The book could only have come from the deep experience of a working forester and the big heart of a gifted writer. Ethan Tapper's book is a love story for our time, beautiful and revolutionary. It left me filled with hope, seeing the forest and the world around me with new eyes."

—Philip Lee, author of *Restigouche:
The Long Run of the Wild River*

"Beautifully written, full of scenes those of us who live in and love the forests of the northeast will recognize immediately."

—Bill McKibben, author of *The End of Nature* and other books

"Rarely has our personal responsibility for the natural world that supports us been so eloquently articulated. Ecological wisdom abounds in Ethan Tapper's story of restoration: wisdom that needs to be spread far, wide, and fast. His ironic yet accurate message? To save a forest, trees need to die. Read this book and find out why."

—Doug Tallamy, author of *Nature's Best Hope*

"With visceral personal experience and a deep sense of history, Ethan Tapper describes the rich life of a forest. Alongside him, we feel the pulse of the Vermont forest at Bear Island as he's working to restore it to health. His book sensitively draws together forest history and social history. The two meet in this personal story of life and place. *How to Love a Forest* is itself a vibrant life and a rich education."

—David A. Taylor, writer, filmmaker, and author of *Ginseng, the Divine Root: The Curious History of the Plant That Captivated the World*

"With strong prose, Ethan Tapper creates an impassioned argument for why each of us should create a more holistic and responsible relationship with our forests—not solely the trees, but the incredible diversity of organisms that exist within them."

—Tom Wessels, author of
Reading the Forested Landscape

HOW TO LOVE A FOREST

HOW TO LOVE A FOREST

the bittersweet work of tending a changing world

ETHAN TAPPER

Broadleaf Books
Minneapolis

HOW TO LOVE A FOREST
The Bittersweet Work of Tending a Changing World

30 29 28 27 26 25 24   4 5 6 7 8 9

Some names have been changed to protect the identity and privacy of individuals.

Library of Congress Cataloging-in-Publication Data

Names: Tapper, Ethan, author.
Title: How to love a forest : the bittersweet work of tending a changing
    world / Ethan Tapper.
Description: Minneapolis, MN : Broadleaf Books, [2024] | Includes
    bibliographical references.
Identifiers: LCCN 2023049182 (print) | LCCN 2023049183 (ebook) | ISBN
    9798889830559 (print) | ISBN 9798889830566 (ebook)
Subjects: LCSH: Tapper, Ethan. | Foresters—Vermont—Biography. | Forests
    and forestry—Vermont—Popular works. | Forest health—Vermont—
    Popular works. | Forest conservation—Vermont—Popular works. |
    Forest ecology—Vermont—Popular works.
Classification: LCC SD129.T356 A3 2024 (print) | LCC SD129.
    T356 (ebook) | DDC 634.909743—dc23/eng/20240131
LC record available at https://lccn.loc.gov/2023049182
LC ebook record available at https://lccn.loc.gov/2023049183

Cover image: © 2023 Getty Images; Multiple exposure of hand, trees and birds/1357830812 by GeorgePeters
Cover design: Juicebox

Print ISBN: 979-8-8898-3055-9
eBook ISBN: 979-8-8898-3056-6

CONTENTS

CONTENTS

INTRODUCTION

Red idles in the dooryard, black smoke rolling into the bright winter air. I climb in, stowing my chainsaw, my oil and gas, my felling wedges and my axe. I grip the worn levers and throw Red into gear. He roars to life, his chain-wrapped tires churning through the snow, carrying me upward into the land that I call Bear Island.

We follow the new trail, threading across the slope. Beside us, the crowns of oaks, sugar maples, and yellow birches reach into the clear sky, treetops and stumps huddled at their feet. We skirt the patch cuts, where acres of young trees pierce the drifting snow, and pass the overlook, where the Skeleton Pine clings to the edge of the cliff. Through her boughs, my eyes trace the course of the big river, flowing steadfastly westward, paralleled by the buzzing highway. We turn north, following the trail through the Big Patch and into the sugar bush.

Red's engine slows to an idle. I climb down from the cab, my chainsaw swinging in my hand. I pause for a moment, listening to the engine purr, the smell of diesel exhaust heavy in the still air. Around me, the forest is settled into the deep quiet of winter. Everything is sleeping.

The last time someone carried a chainsaw through the snow here, they walked toward the largest trees, mythical creatures

1

now remembered only by their stumps. The last time a skidder like Red idled on this trail, it was a tool used to pull dollars from this forest, no matter the cost. I have not gentled these beasts, only turned them toward the hope of a different future. On this day, the skidder and the chainsaw are tools of healing, channeled toward life.

I stop in front of a beech tree, its trunk rising between two little sugar maples. The beech is stunted and contorted, a legacy of the loggers who "high-graded" this forest, cutting all its healthiest trees and leaving all its least healthy trees behind. Its bark is cracked and pockmarked by beech bark disease, a nonnative pathogen introduced to this forest decades ago. In the beech's shade, the sugar maples shine in the winter light, their branches reaching toward the hope of a better future. I know that they will not reach it without my help.

I lay a gloved hand on the beech's trunk. As the chainsaw idles beside me, a part of me wants the beech to live, to believe that this forest will thrive even if I do nothing. It is not true. In this changed and changing world, we are offered choices that are nuanced and unclear, bittersweet and shadowed with compromise. I remind myself that there is nothing radical about doing what is easy and convenient and comfortable, nothing radical about doing nothing. I remind myself that what is truly radical is to do what is necessary to build a better world.

I brace the saw and pull it to life.

I grew up in a small town in southeastern Vermont, surrounded by mountains, forests, and rivers. Though forests were ever-present in my life, it never occurred to me that they were my calling—that I would someday become a forester.

My journey toward forests and forestry began in college. After drifting through two aimless semesters at the University of Vermont, I left to follow a woman I loved on a wilderness expedition through the woods of New England. I spent the next six months living in the woods—traveling by ski and canoe, sleeping on a floor of fir boughs, spending days under the sun and nights under the stars.

One day in early March, our little group of twelve carried our skis up a steep mountain highway. We passed a washed-out gravel road, a rusted cable with a worn *Keep Out* sign pulled across its entrance. Though I did not realize it until many years later, we walked past a place that I would someday give my life to, a place that would teach me what it means to love a forest, a place that I would someday call Bear Island.

Two months later, we were strong and tan. We canoed south as the beaked hazelnuts flaunted their tiny pink flowers, slivers of ice and snow still hiding in the hollows of the forest. As we traced the course of the long river, the world slowly awakened. By the end of May, ostrich ferns decorated the floodplains. The forest was green and bright, ephemeral wildflowers glowing on the flanks of the mountains.

As summer bloomed, we were back at basecamp, spending our last weeks together constructing a timber frame barn. As we shaped hemlock beams and hoisted them into place we were joyful and embodied, in the afterglow of a transformative journey. The forest had become a home to me: in the evenings, I would walk through the woods and wetlands around our camp, watching the birds feeding their chicks and the beavers building their dams, feeling a sense of belonging and connection. My world felt massive and expansive and also small and soft and warm.

On a humid June morning, I climbed onto the scaffolding. I felt the warm and pregnant summer air on my skin as I cranked the come-along, pulling a post and beam together until they settled into one another. I listened to my friends' chatter, the creak of the timbers, the groan of the come-along as the rope tightened and tightened further. I pulled the lever again, and the rope snapped.

I only remember my ears ringing. Blood falling onto the timbers. My left side instantly cast into darkness.

I said, "I can't see out of my left eye." And then I was being carried off the scaffolding, loaded into a truck and then an ambulance, carried to one hospital and then another, rushed into surgery, awakening under fluorescent lights at dusk. I soon learned that I would live, but that my left eye would be blinded forever.

In the year after my accident, I was called toward darkness, wandering a landscape of pain, loss, and depression. I could not tell the distances between things. I could not cross the river, jumping from stone to stone. I stood in the aftermath of a windstorm, in the ashes of a wildfire, the forest of my life irrevocably changed. I was lost.

Forests became my refuge. I spent the years that followed among the plants and the trees and the animals: practicing tracking, bushcraft, and traditional skills, working as a wilderness guide. In a confusing, painful, and disjointed world, I saw forests as places of balance, utopias, perfect communities. To me, loving the forest meant leaving it alone, and the people who changed it, who took from it, were my antagonists. I was dogmatic, believing that I had discovered the only truly compassionate relationship with the forest. There was no room in my mind for any other way of being.

After two years in the woods, I was told that if I did not return to the university the following semester I would lose my scholarship. I shuddered, remembering the lights and the buildings of the city, the paved roads and the chattering people, the classrooms of children in adult clothes. I sat on my yurt's bough floor, the woodstove simmering beside me, and scanned the list of degrees, wondering what, if anything, was worth my time. All I knew about forestry was that it had the word *forest* in it, but that was enough.

In September I returned to the world of people, feeling like a bear in a suit. I immersed myself in dendrology, botany, biology, soil science, chemistry, geology, natural history—the many disciplines that combine to describe the expansive living system that is a forest. Even as my courses divided ecosystems into pieces and parts, I found stories and patterns, repeated and intertwined, living threads binding them together. I learned to reimagine forests as complex, dynamic communities, defined by connection and relationship, enriched by death and change.

I learned that the forests I had once considered "perfect" and "pristine" were actually altered and unhealthy: shuddering in the midst of a climate crisis and a biodiversity crisis, wounded by the legacies of the past and facing one incredible challenge after another, caged within the countless subtle imbalances that pervaded this earth. Slowly, I began to understand the beauty of action, to reimagine what it meant to truly love a forest.

I learned to use a chainsaw and spent a summer apprenticed to a draft horse logger in Maine. Each day, I watched as dozens of pines and hemlocks trembled, tipped, and thundered indelicately to the ground. Each day, I walked the lengths of the felled trees, slicing logs from their long trunks. Each day, I hitched the horses to the logs and skidded them to the landing, the leather reins light in my hardening hands. At the end of each week, as darkness settled over the forest, the horses and I would be lathered in sweat, watching the trucker stack tiers of pine and hemlock logs between the trailer's steel staves.

In the mornings, I would walk through the changed forest with my chainsaw on my shoulder. I would step over pine boughs and around shattered treetops, would cross the stark light of the new gaps opened in the forest's canopy. The managed forest felt raw and unfamiliar and also profound: a beautiful mess, full of light and life and promise. I began to see that there were no endings here: that the light slanting to the forest floor was destined to manifest a generation of young trees and plants, that the stumps and the treetops were destined to become homes to bustling communities of mosses and lichens, fungi and bacteria, insects and salamanders, bears and butterflies. I began to see that the spaces between the trees were as full and as beautiful as the trees themselves.

As I started the chainsaw again, I remembered the person I had been: the person who was so certain that leaving forests alone made him radical and progressive. Suddenly, this person seemed blind to the realities of the world, lacking the courage and the vision to help the forests that he claimed to love. Suddenly, he seemed like a child with his hands over his ears, fighting for nothing as the world burned around him.

The chainsaw purred in my hands. I asked myself if a better world would be built by inaction or by relationship and responsibility. I asked myself, *What is the cost of doing nothing?*

I graduated college and took a job as a consulting forester, working on private and industrial forests in Vermont, New Hampshire, and Maine. After five years, I took a job with the State of Vermont as a service forester, tasked with helping private landowners understand how to care for their forests.

In 2017, eight years after my accident, I bought a piece of land on the mountain road and named it Bear Island. To me, Bear Island was a symbol of what the world had become: crooked and strange, broken and unjust and incomplete, two hundred acres of degraded and mismanaged forest, unhealthy trees, rutted skid trails, and nonnative invasive plants. It was also a call to action—a living community of depth and value that could not move forward on its own.

As I explored the radical actions necessary to help Bear Island become healthy and vibrant again, I began to truly understand how forest management could be restorative and regenerative, how it could enrich forests, how it could help forests rediscover their true capacity for life. I began to truly understand how the cutting of a tree could be an expression of compassion and humility, an act of healing, an act of love.

Once, it seemed that there were only two paths to follow: a status quo that saw forests and other ecosystems as commodities, and an opposing force that sought to protect ecosystems from ourselves, to leave them alone. As forests everywhere struggle under the weight of the many threats and stressors of the modern world, as they suffer the legacies of the past and confront a future that promises challenges like never before, Bear Island has helped me realize that neither of these two paths is enough. I have realized that the world needs action intertwined with compassion, relationship imbued with responsibility, death infused with life. I have gone my own way, fostering a divergent vision—a reimagining of what it means to love a forest. As I manage Bear Island, I engage in the radical act of trading simplicity for complexity, trading a tidy vision for one that is true.

My journey toward these realizations has been long and lonely and sinuous. In my little house at the foot of the mountain, my bookshelf is crowded with books about trees and plants and animals, birds and bears and fungi, the relationship between people and ecosystems and the threats both face. Never have I found a book that has articulated what a forest truly is—not just its botany and its biology, the contours of its many pieces and its parts, but how this entire living community moves and behaves and changes. Never have I found a book that described what it means to care for a forest like Bear Island, an ecosystem that has been changed and degraded and depleted and left to suffer alone. Never have I found a book that described the pain and the joy and the anxiety of trying to love and protect an ecosystem, of guiding it toward wholeness at this strange and a crucial moment in time. No book has prepared me for the many complex and bittersweet choices that I would someday make at Bear Island, or for the fact that these actions would be celebrations, the substance of a truly radical and responsible relationship with a forest.

Finally, nowhere have I found a book that recognized that forests are *socioecological* systems—that our lives are forever stitched into the green flesh of the biosphere, that the separation of the human world from the wild world is an illusion. We cannot care for ecosystems without recognizing that we will always rely on them and we will always tax them, that human life will always be precious and worth nourishing and will always come at a cost. We cannot choose *if* we will impact ecosystems, *if* we will impact peoples across the globe, *if* we will impact the lives of future generations. We can only choose what that impact will be.

In this book I draw these disparate threads together, exploring what it means to love a forest in this changed and changing world. It is a new land ethic, a vision of relationship and responsibility, freedom and power, resilience and humility, legacy, beauty, and change: themes that define my life and my work and that became the basis for this book's chapters. In a world that is both human and wild, both wounded and vibrant, both suppressed and emergent, this is a vision both for how we manage forests and take care of ecosystems and how we manage ourselves, how we take care of each other.

I hope this book will give others the courage to engage in the bittersweet work of tending this changing world, so that others will not have to walk this same path alone.

The beech creaks and shudders, the slice from the saw widening. It hangs for a moment and then crashes to earth, throwing a cloud of powder into the dry air. I turn off the saw, my breath ragged and heavy in my ears.

The beech lies in the snow like a queen in her coffin. A moment ago this was a living being, elegant and regal and many decades my senior, a tree that rose above thousands of others to rule a slender tract of this blue sky. Even as she succumbed to beech bark disease, the beech tree was a refuge in a foreboding world: casting rich seeds around her, nurturing countless flying and crawling and growing things. She survived the logger's saws, for a time even surviving the pathogen that turned her smooth bark into a moonscape of black cobbles. In death, the beech will be here still. The legacies of her passing, as precious and as impactful as her life, will resonate through the forest forever.

The sugar maples sway, their brown leaders suddenly liberated. Next spring, they will expand from every edge, reaching their crowns outward and upward, thickening their whitewashed trunks. As the sugar maples grow, the death of the beech will be revealed as an act of generation. The sugar maples will remind me that my work is not about destroying a world that is broken; it is about building a world that is beautiful.

One day I will tap the sugar maples, will boil their sap into maple syrup so that life may be a little sweeter. I will lay my hand on their trunks and remember that is not enough to survive this moment. I want to thrive, to manifest a world as rich and as sweet as maple syrup.

I hug a chain around the beech and hitch it to Red's silvery cable. I am many contradictory things at once, a revolutionary in a world that demands consistency and simplicity: if I love trees I must not cut trees, if I love forests I must leave forests alone. Somehow, the beech and the sugar maples are both part of the same radical vision: a forest that is a community of intrinsic value, a forest that is inexorably linked to the human world, a forest that I need and that needs me, now more than ever. Somehow, both are expressions of love.

Snow crystals flicker in the fading light. I climb into the cab and engage the winch, pulling the beech like a fish on a line, leaving ripples in the snow. In the spring the beech will be bucked, split, and stacked. The two little maples will reach upward, emboldened, becoming queens in their own right.

We already have the tools to save this world—we just need to choose to do so. There is no turning back the clock; there is only this moment, filled with doubt and anxiety and promise. There is no one coming to save us; only ourselves, imperfect and powerful and imbued with responsibility. There are no perfect solutions; only endless bittersweet compromises, choices that dare us to reimagine what it means to live in this world with compassion. There is so much that is wrong and so much worth saving.

I turn toward my little house, where the wood stove creaks and whirrs and the light slants through the big south windows, where the maple syrup glows in the jar on the table. I steer the roaring skidder down the hill through the snow.

1 | REIMAGINING: OUR FORESTS, OURSELVES

The cold presses against my cheeks, sinking into the hollows around my eyes. I strap on my snowshoes and head up the unplowed road.

Though the forest is quiet, I know that it is alive. Between the boulders of Stimson Mountain the bear sows sleep, their cubs nursing and mewling like kittens. Rodents tunnel through the *subnivean zone*, the cavernous world beneath the snow, hunted by foxes and owls and ermine weasels. Deer linger in the hemlocks in their shaggy winter coats, and grouse leave wingbeats on the snow. The trees stand nakedly above it all, next year's growth promised in every closed bud.

The round tracks of a moose merge onto the road ahead of me, and I picture a big bull fumbling up the hill, his fleshy bell bobbing with each postholing step. Somewhere on the mountain, that moose chews yellow birch twigs, waiting to wade in warm waters again. The road curls to the north and flattens. I enter the long, narrow clearing, the yurt squatting like an acorn at its center. I am here again.

I glide to the blue trailer, the miniature camper surrounded by useful things and precious things and things with nowhere else to go. Under the snow, I can see the rounded shapes of the upside-down wheelbarrow, the old culvert, the wooden stepladder, the disassembled car port, piles of scrap steel, fencing, buckets, and thick slabs of wood. Behind the trailer's red door are shovels, saws, and axes, a bear hide that I keep failing to tan but cannot throw away. A few months ago, mice ruined my generator, and so now there are mouse traps on every surface, baited with frozen peanut butter.

The broken ridge of Stimson Mountain leans over me, shining with white winter light. One day this place, Bear Island, will be my home. Today, I am just a weekend visitor from an apartment in Burlington, an interloper in this wild world. I grab my pruning shears and point my snowshoes toward the orchard, where the fruit trees wait in the snow.

As is my custom, I take a detour up the path to the pond. Three years ago, when I bought Bear Island, the pond was a snarl of skidder ruts, a wallow of soupy black muck. Now green water gathers under the ice, cattails piercing its shallows. The pond has become a place where herons wade on their stilts, where black bears drink in summer. Somewhere in its belly, a school of trout live out their lives, their flanks pink, their glassy eyes bulging. I built the pond so that I could swim and stocked it with trout so that I could fish, but now what brings me the most joy is just knowing that both are here.

From the top of the dam, I turn to face my young orchard. The trees are little more than saplings, a constellation of tiny stars. Three years ago, I planted these trees among stumps and brush, the brown slash of the clearing simmering around them. Apples, pears, cherries, and chestnuts, their roots naked to the summer air, were thrust into holes in the sandy soil, the auger's blade choking on roots and rocks. Each year I plant another apple or pear, another plum, another bright peach. More trees will arrive in April, sealed in a long cardboard box.

The clearing is far from an ideal place for an orchard. Thirteen thousand years ago, I would have stood on the shore of a massive glacial lake, its waters swirling around my feet. For two millennia, the lake filled western Vermont, covering land sunken from tens of thousands of years trapped under a glacier. For two millennia, the lake turned mountains into islands, valleys into long fingers of icy water. Thirteen thousand years ago, I could have turned south and walked over the broad valley, my snowshoes carrying me hundreds of feet above where the highway now sings its ceaseless song, where towns and villages cluster, where the big river blinks its slow, green eyes. Beneath the blue ice, tiny soil particles would have drifted like stray hairs, catching the light. Over thousands of years, they gathered: sands and gravels on the lake's deltas and shorelines, clays filtering through its deeper waters.

Eleven thousand years ago, far to the north, the last memories of the glacier failed, its dam of ice suddenly breached. The lake rushed out of the broad valley, leaving this flat plateau, this sandy beach with no ocean stranded on the side of the mountain. Over thousands of years, the brook gnawed downward through sand and gravel, shaping the plateau's eastern edge until it was as curved as an hourglass. Today that same brook rushes hundreds of feet below, its currents wearing caverns in the bedrock.

Over the succeeding millennia, the plateau's soils developed in a process that was both organic and inorganic, both prescribed and unpredictable, both known and unknowable. As the

memories of an ice age receded from the broad valley, the plateau became a tundra, a taiga, a forest one hundred times over.
Roots plumbed the soil's depths, twisting and diving in the dark,
carrying communities of tiny things in their arms. Over unthinkable spans of time, the soil's minerals were mined by fungi and
bacteria, weathered by water and time, transformed physically,
chemically, and biologically. Countless windstorms crossed the
plateau, and the structure and the composition of its forest were
changed in broad, sweeping strokes; again and again, the trees
fell, their root systems lifting the dark topsoil and exposing the
orange gravel beneath, turning the soil like hands in dough.
Again and again, the forest regenerated, chasing death with life.
Fires singed the soil's upper reaches, some kindled by the first
people of the valley, who crossed the plateau as they hunted elk
and moose and caribou, their birch bark canoes beached on the
shores of the big river far below. Slowly, the plateau's soil deepened and darkened and changed.

Two centuries ago, a village of colonists bloomed at the foot
of the mountain. The plateau and the mountain above were
cleared and pastured, the forest exiled and kept at bay for a century or more. The plateau was home to the village's baseball
field, and on humid summer evenings the children of the valley
would hike up the shoulders of the brook with their caps and
their leather gloves, playing baseball as the sun ebbed behind the
crooked ridge of Stimson Mountain.

Three decades ago, the plateau had been ignored by the
people of the valley for generations. Miraculously, it had regenerated, becoming a young forest of oak and beech, red maple
and pine. One day, the people returned to the plateau and began
to clear the young forest again. They made a round clearing at

the plateau's southern end, dug a small gravel pit, built a steep, curving road that connected the plateau to the pavement below. For the decade that followed, the clearing was a log landing: the place where loggers parked their pickups as they rode roaring skidders to every corner of the mountain, where they stacked endless tiers of oak and maple logs, where they loaded hundreds of log trucks and sent them to the mill. One day in late autumn, the soils of the clearing were slick and muddy, and so a logger in a bulldozer scraped away what was left of the black topsoil, piling it on the edges of the clearing, exposing the orange gravel again.

From atop the pond's dam, the topsoil is a faint bulge under the snow, ringing the margins of the clearing. At the clearing's southern end, the gravel pit is an open mouth, slicing through ten feet of gravel and into a pool of soft white sand, fine enough to be caught by the wind. When I first came to Bear Island, the clearing's soils—soils that had once been rich and deep and ancient—were depleted and compacted, barely able to grow tufts of thin, yellow grass. The clearing was piled with trash; cables and hydraulic hoses and oil buckets buried like poison seeds in the earth. To the north, what remained of the plateau's forest was a tangle of skidder ruts, its trees anemic and half-alive, the spaces between them empty. After thirteen thousand years of reaching toward life, the plateau seemed transparent: a place that was less than nothing.

I exhale. Tiny ice crystals drift through the air like shoals of plankton, flickering in the low winter light. This clearing on the plateau, like this world, is a map of scars. I have begun to build something on the rubble of the past, but I know that this is no beginning. The clearing still remembers the crush of the glacier and the icy waters that followed. It remembers the forests that have lived here, the many worlds that have called this place their home. It remembers the pasture and the ball field, the log landing and the bulldozer. My life is just the latest chapter in an endless history, a brief moment on the edge of a massive skein of time.

I descend the dam and walk through the orchard, tracing the tracks of mice on the snow. My trees reach defiantly upward, each protected by a circle of wire fence. Once these trees were seedlings in a nursery, a place closer to a farm than a forest. One winter, their tips were severed and replaced with slender lengths of scionwood, cultivars chosen by human hands. Somehow, they healed, the scionwood and rootstock of each fusing until they became a single entity, a composite being. Months passed and they were uprooted again, shipped over miles of shining road and planted by my hands on the shores of an extinct glacial lake.

Somehow these trees have taken root in the compacted, dry, acidic, soil, this legacy of so many varied and unimaginable things. Somehow their trunks have swelled, their branches reaching a little higher and a little farther each year. Somehow these trees have survived the early days of the orchard, when I neglected them and they were browsed by deer, bent by snow, nibbled by meadow voles, baked by the scalding summer sun. They have suffered my forester's distrust of trees that need to be coddled, and they have shown their resilience. They want to live.

Beneath the frozen soil, the trees' roots wait for the thaw, for another summer of searching blindly and purposefully through the earth. They are not doing it alone. Microscopic threads of *mycorrhizal fungi* branch like watersheds from their root tips, miles of hyphae in a pinch of soil. The orchard trees and the fungi are engaged in an ancient *mutualism*: the fungi channeling minerals and water into the trees' roots, the trees returning a tithe of the sugars that their leaves produce.

Around the trees' roots, the *rhizosphere*, the world of roots, blooms: a community of bacteria, invertebrates, and free-living fungi. As with the mycorrhizal fungi, the trees subsidize the creatures of the rhizosphere: sending precious sugars, in the form of *root exudates*, flooding into the soil so that they may feast. As with the mycorrhizal fungi, the trees receive something vital in return: as the creatures of the rhizosphere live their cryptic lives, they unlock the riches of the soil, transforming critical nutrients like nitrogen into forms that the trees can use.

In two months, against all odds, leaves will unfold from every bud, feathering these trees in green. Each leaf on every tree will effortlessly enact a process honed over eons of deep time: *photosynthesis*, the engine of this living world. Photosynthesis is the legacy of another ancient mutualism: the bonding of chloroplasts, once independent organisms, into the cells of living plants. Through the miracle of photosynthesis, plants turn four nonliving things—light, air, water, earth—into living tissue, guiding matter across the threshold from abiotic to biotic, from inert to alive. In the process, trees and plants respire oxygen and water vapor, seeding our atmosphere with breathable air and painting our skies with rain clouds. In two months, each leaf on every tree in the orchard will turn toward the sun, repeating the process that has made life, in all its colors, possible.

I approach my Golden Delicious and begin to prune, its fine twigs disappearing into the snow. The winter air slices through my layers of wool, touching my pink skin. Within my tender body, warm red blood rushes through watersheds of veins, from my beating heart to the tips of my numb fingers. Oxygen exhaled by plants saturates my twin lungs as they expand and contract. Carbon pulled from the atmosphere by green leaves nourishes me, giving my body the means to breathe, to stay warm, to move through the snow. Like this apple tree, I am a wild thing—a product of the *biosphere*, the thin veneer of life that surrounds this planet. Like this apple tree, I am also something apart, something bred and pruned and planted. Whatever I am, I cannot live alone—like every living thing, I cannot exist without forests, without plants, without water, without soil.

I prune a finger of diseased wood from the Golden Delicious, placing it on the pile to be removed and burned. In the orchard I struggle against stressors and pests, against death and decline, going to great measures to keep each of these trees alive and healthy. Above me, the wild trees on the flanks of the mountain face their own mortal struggles. As I fuss over the trees in the orchard, the trees on the mountain weather parasites and pathogens, drought and inundation, the many perils that must be endured by something rooted in place.

In the orchard, the bacteria, the fungi, the boring and defoliating insects are villains, threats to the order and the productivity of this engineered system. In the forest they are the *necrosphere*: the community of death, the midwives of the profound and beautiful process of tree mortality, the creatures that guide trees toward the unraveling that marks the end of their biological lives. The trees of the forest are members of a community that has evolved in a world of windstorms and ice storms and forest fires, of insect and disease outbreaks, a community that has been defoliated and parasitized, broken and uprooted, burned and flooded for millennia. As I fight death in the orchard, the trees of the forest will live and die with equanimity.

In the forest, the creatures of the necrosphere are as natural and as essential as the trees themselves; beings of value and purpose, critical pieces of a living system in which death is as vital as life. As they kill trees, they create nests and dens, fertile seedbeds for mosses and lichens and young trees, habitats for countless species. As they rot and break down wood, the creatures of the necrosphere build and enrich soils, making future generations of trees possible.

Last year, I led a group from a local senior center to one of Vermont's few remaining old-growth forests, a few acres in the heart of the Champlain Valley. The group murmured contentedly as we entered a stand of sugar maple trees, their trunks small and perfect, the crowns of white pines looming far overhead. It was October, and the sugar maple leaves were drifting lazily to the ground, the color of burnt gold. I smiled as I explained that this was not the old-growth forest—that, like most of Vermont, this beautiful stand of trees had been a pasture just sixty years before.

Ahead, the old-growth forest loomed darkly, its understory a tangle of fallen trees and dense young growth, its canopy layered and irregular and punctuated by gaps, its oldest trees hollow and half-dead. As we entered, the autumn light faded into shadow. From behind me, I heard a quavering voice say, "Oh, I don't like that."

In my time as a forester, I have walked in the woods with many hundreds of people. I have realized that each of us is drawn to forests like orchards: forests that are simple and tidy, defined and discrete, bounded and finite. Our intuition guides us to envision healthy forests as expanses of evenly spaced trees towering over understories as clear and as open as parks. Research suggests that this bias may be evolutionary in nature—that we are drawn toward savanna-like environments, analogs of the African ecosystems within which our species evolved for millions of years. Like every species on earth, we reach toward suitable habitat, instincts hardened in forgotten times singing from the backs of our minds.

If a group of ecologists and biologists walked through the same old-growth forest, they would marvel at its *structural diversity*: how natural disturbances of different types and scales had created a mosaic of young trees and old trees, young forest and old forest and everything in between. They would smile at the broken snags standing like huge naked obelisks, at the trunks of fallen trees piled at their feet, at the ancient trees inhabiting the *perimortem period*: the rich, liminal space between life and death. They would celebrate the forest for the same reasons that made the group from the senior center so uncomfortable—its messiness, its imperfections, the legacies of death and the change that defined it. They would see the old-growth forest as a vibrant, dynamic community with a radical vision of what it means to thrive.

A group of chickadees visits me, flitting from fence to fence. I pause to watch their circus. As my pruning shears quiet, I hear nuthatches and dark-eyed juncos, the pounding of a pileated woodpecker on an aspen. As I have learned to recognize more of the forest's birds, a cacophony has become a chorus. Each species of bird calls its own name. Each touches the forest in a different way, each finding habitat within different pieces and parts of this living community. Each is unique.

A decade ago, I looked into the forest and saw faceless trees, each like the others. As I learned to tell sugar maple from red maple, the flat needles of hemlock from the angular needles of spruce, the peeling bark of paper birch from the creamy bark of aspen, the forest has become a creature of diversity and complexity and depth. Each tree species is habitat for different birds, insects, and mammals, each growing on different sites and in different ways, each flourishing different flowers and bearing different fruits. Each is precious.

Once, I saw forests as no different from orchards. I have since learned to reimagine the forest as something messy and imperfect, complex and undefinable, dynamic and expansive over space and time. I have learned to see the trees in the forest as the coral in a coral reef, the living structure at the center of a community of boundless depth and diversity.

I have learned that an understanding of what healthy forests look like, how they work, and what it means to take care of them is not something that any of us are born with; it is something we need to develop. I have learned that forests are not supposed to be pleasant or understandable or beautiful to us. They are what they are, and it is up to us to meet them there.

Now, when I look into the forest, I see kaleidoscopes of interactions and connections, critical pieces and parts as diminutive as a bed of moss on a rotting log and as massive as a mountain, a region, a continent, a biosphere. Now, I see that the fungi and the bacteria of the soil, the insects, the mosses and the lichens, the beech and the oak, the deer and the owls and the bears: these things do not *live* in the forest—they *are* the forest. The windstorms and the ice storms, the forest fires and the floods, the death and the change: these things do not *happen* to the forest—they *are* the forest. Once I thought that being a forester meant being a caretaker of trees. Now I see myself as the caretaker of a reimagined forest, the steward of every piece of this incredible volume of life.

I begin pruning again, my shears cutting away the dead wood and the water sprouts, the branches that cross one another and those that face downward. Though I have learned to appreciate the beauty of messiness, I am still soothed by the order and the simplicity of a pruned tree. I still smile when I walk through the orchard in summer, the trees standing in perfect rows, the grass cropped low between them. In the orchard, I manifest a human dream, a vision of uniformity, efficiency, and productivity. To the west, the forest on the mountain lives its own dream: enigmatic and messy and strange, thousands of species of living things inhabiting patterns and processes and relationships honed over millennia. Though a piece of me aches to spread the order of the orchard up the slopes of the mountain, I know that to do so would be a great injustice.

It has not always been this way—historically, forests have often been managed more like orchards than like complex, living systems. In the early 1900s, the first North American foresters practiced "scientific forestry"—a system of growing timber quickly and efficiently, often within the context of intensively managed conifer plantations. Scientific forestry was a discipline of command and control, based on an ethic that saw trees as crops to be harvested and forests as factories of timber and fiber. Embedded within scientific forestry was the notion of *the regulated forest*: the idea that every aspect of a forest could and should be controlled, engineered to produce wood as quickly and efficiently as possible.

At a time when forests across this continent were largely managed without any regard for the future, scientific foresters believed that they were moving forward: replacing wanton exploitation with intentionality and thoughtfulness. Yet, as they tried to provide timber for a growing world, they failed to recognize that forests are more than timber. As they managed forests to be tidy and orderly and uncomplicated, they failed to see that forests' true riches are found in messiness and complexity, diversity and dynamism—that to remove these ingredients was to undermine forests' resilience and their vibrance, their health, their wealth, their beauty. As the scientific foresters managed forests like orchards, they failed to see that the inefficiencies and imperfections, the necrosphere and the rhizosphere, the wildlife and the plants, the natural disturbances, are as much a part of healthy forests as the trees.

I stand back to look at the Golden Delicious, its branches half naked. I picture the scientific foresters, walking through the forest in their three-piece suits, replacing the chaos of a natural forest with monocultures of trees in straight rows. I picture them killing beautiful old "decadent" trees to make space for faster-growing, more valuable "thrifty" trees, trading diversity and complexity for efficiency and productivity. As they managed forests like numbers on a ledger, I imagine that the scientific foresters believed they were doing something truly evolved: turning a wild thing into something refined and civilized. In truth, they were doing something truly primitive: transforming forests into savannas, managing a living system to comply with their most primal instincts.

Today, many people understand that forests are not commodities—that they are worth so much more than the timber they produce. However, many have traded the misconceptions of scientific forestry for a new raft of misunderstandings. Research has shown that the mycorrhizal fungi that infuses the soil beneath the snow can span the root systems of different trees, trees of different generations, even trees of different species, forming *common mycorrhizal networks*. Other research has suggested that, through these networks, trees may share resources and communicate with one another; that old trees may "subsidize" younger trees; healthy trees may share resources with stressed trees; dying trees may funnel resources to surviving trees. Because of these purported properties, these mycorrhizal networks have been nicknamed "the Wood Wide Web."

As I make another cut with the pruning shears, I think of how the idea of the Wood Wide Web has led many to appreciate and to value forests in a new way. I think, too, of how it has seeded a new array of misconceptions about them. As people have learned more about relationship, communication, and even altruism between trees, they have mythologized forests, thinking of them as utopias, and anthropomorphized trees, thinking of them as people. In forests built on competition, parasitism, and predation as much as on communication and collaboration, on death as much as on life, people have imagined that forests are gardens of peaceful and perfect relationships.

Today, while we know that mycorrhizal fungi may, and often do, have mutualistic relationships with trees, the resource-sharing, communication, and many of the other qualities once attributed to the Wood Wide Web are considered speculative at best. A recent analysis of the research about common mycorrhizal networks has revealed a systemic bias toward the idea of the Wood Wide Web: that even some researchers have ignored alternate explanations and clear knowledge gaps in favor of this exciting concept.

Above me, the creatures of the forest on the mountain, like the people of the world, awaken each day to the thrill of survival, their lives open to trauma, love, prejudice, and opportunity. They collaborate and compete, oppress each other and lift each other up, raise children and mourn the dead, leave legacies for the world of the future. Perhaps each tree in this forest is a small part of a single, massive organism, a hair on the head of an ancient and expansive being. Perhaps not. Today, the Wood Wide Web is an exciting idea, nothing more. The truth of it is less important to me than what I do to protect and enrich the life of this precious community, its present and its future, all its pieces and parts.

I think of the scientific foresters and the proponents of the Wood Wide Web, wondering if it is more beautiful to weave fantasies around forests or to have the humility to see them as they truly are. I wonder if we could find the humility to love a forest not because it is easy but because it is difficult; not because it is simple but because it is complex, not because it is like us but because it is so different.

The winter light shines through the open crown of the Golden Delicious. The purpose of this tree is simple: to grow, to spread its crown, to one day produce fruit that I will pick and eat. The forest on the mountain above has no purpose, no goal to achieve. It exists to exist—to live, to die, to change—and that is enough. It dares me to understand.

I start pruning the large limbs at the center of my Red Rome apple, moving outward until I am holding the tip of each branch, shaping and steering one tiny bud and twig at a time. With each cut I make order out of chaos, turning a tangle of branches into something understandable and uncomplicated. Somehow this tree is thriving, its twigs capped in fat, silver buds, the cuts from last year's pruning wrapped in crescents of purple scar tissue.

Above me, the forest on the mountain is a miracle of resilience. Like nearly all New England's forests, an ancient forest was cleared from this mountain two centuries ago, its snags felled, its dead wood burned or dragged away. One hundred years ago, the mountain was an abandoned pasture, its sod just beginning to roughen with goldenrod and meadowsweet, its winding cattle paths softening and callousing over. The trees that now rule the forest's canopy were tiny seedlings, their leaves brushing blades of yellow grass.

Today, one hundred years since the forest on the mountain was a pasture, thirty years since loggers cut nearly all its largest trees, most people would walk the mountain's many skid trails and assume this forest was ageless and primeval. They would not know that this forest is as altered as an orchard. They would not know that it is young and simple and vulnerable, abused and on the brink of collapse, shaped by oppression and degradation and loss.

In a world of young, simple forests, we experience *shifting baseline syndrome*: the belief that the things we are used to are normal. In fact, the forest on the mountain and the forests of our world are aberrations, oddities, unprecedented and unfamiliar; shining replicas standing in place of ancient relics. The forest on the mountain misses its structural diversity, its dead wood, its ancient trees, the conditions around which the members of its biological community built their lives and their evolutionary identities for millennia. To the birds and the moose, the deer and the bear, the ants and the butterflies, the minnows and the tree frogs, these losses are as real and as tangible as missing limbs. So much of this ecosystem has been lost. So much is still missing.

Next summer, I will fell a beech tree on the mountain, tearing a gap in the forest's canopy. In the coming years, the forest community will seize this moment as it has for millennia, filling this space with life like water flowing to the low places of the earth. Flowering plants will bloom in the light, beetles and flies hanging from their soft petals. Raspberries and blackberries will sprout from seeds that have lain dormant in the soil for decades, and a black bear will sit among them, gorging itself on sweet, dark fruit. Songbirds will nest in the gap's green thickets and dart overhead, catching insects on the wing. In five years, the body of the beech will be colonized by fungi and infused with arthropods, tiny hemlocks sinking their roots into its softening trunk. Thousands of seedlings of dozens of different tree species will race upward toward the hole in the canopy, each reaching toward its own destiny. The tragedy of death will be lost in the abundance of life.

Over the coming years, I will fell thousands of trees. I will engage in endless bittersweet compromises, doing what is necessary to help the forest on the mountain become a little more diverse, a little more complex, a little more resilient, a little more like an ancient forest each year.

At the end of my life, I hope that I will have helped this living community rediscover a capacity for life that it has not known for centuries, an abundance that the people of the valley have not known for seven generations. At the end of my life, the forest will not care whether it was a windstorm or a chainsaw that felled the beech tree. All that will matter is that it happened, and that it is good.

This summer, scaffolds of tender wood will spread between the Red Rome's branches. My pruning will be undone as this living thing becomes a forest in miniature: defying order, reaching toward complexity, filling space with life. Next March I will prune it again.

By the time I am an old man, I will have pruned this tree dozens of times. As the drama of the beech is repeated again and again across the mountain, the trees in the orchard will hang heavy with fruit, their bodies built of countless tiny scars.

It is hard to walk away from an apple tree with the pruning shears in my hand. I circle my Baldwin again and again, each time finding another cut to make. I remember what an old-timer once told me: that you should prune an apple tree until you can "throw a cat through it." The trees in my orchard will be too small to throw a cat through for years to come, but I will guide them on their way—pruning and training them until they are as open and symmetrical as candelabras, light and air flowing evenly to each branch, each with a distinct purpose and direction.

Under the snow, Bear Island awaits another spring. The first time that I visited this land, it seemed beyond hope, orphaned by the modern world. When I returned a second time, I found beauty hiding behind its scars—so many things worth saving. The forest on the mountain has lived many lives: once old growth, once sheep pasture, once woodlot. As the world darkens, the forest persists, holding no grudges. Now, it is fated to become something else. I will help it on its way.

The westerly wind sweeps across the mountain, and the cold touches me again. I shiver. For years I held a secret dream: a piece of land, a homestead, a forest of my own. My dream has come true, but it is different than I imagined. I have been gifted and burdened with a forest as cracked and as crooked as this biosphere, wounded and troubled, facing an impossible future. The forest on the mountain grows into a climate crisis and a biodiversity crisis, into a world that has lost so many pieces of itself, a world in which it seems that everything is breaking and everything precious is under threat. This land is vital and tender and wounded; it offers me freedom infused with profound responsibility. It is not enough to prune the trees in my orchard, to follow my ambition toward a personal peace. My dream has changed.

For this slender moment in time, I am the caretaker of both an orchard and a forest, of a parcel of land that is both human and wild, both a universe of its own and a fragment of a complex reality. I wonder how this land and I will change across the swells of my short life, what parts of ourselves we may discover and rediscover and reimagine.

I return the loppers to the frozen chaos of the trailer and head down the hill, crossing the moose tracks, softened by the midday sun. I consider my own legacy: the world I am manifesting at Bear Island with all this work and time and energy, all this thought and care and frustration. I dream that my future children and grandchildren will know Bear Island not as an expression of dysfunction but as a beacon of hope, vibrant and abundant. I dream that this land will be a candle that catches the world on fire, a small, vital organ in the body of a world that is functional and beautiful, just and kind.

Someday the apple trees in the orchard will bloom, and bees will visit their white flowers. Wild plants will grow at the apples' feet, and nuthatches will search for insects in the ravines and slot canyons of their flaking bark. On summer nights, bats will flit across the red sky, and in November deer will paw the half-frozen ground, searching for forgotten apples. Someday, the leaves of the orchard will have become an arching canopy and I will sit in their shade with a grandchild on my knee, listening to the buzzing of the bees and eating crisp, golden apples. Today, it is enough to begin.

As I descend the last slope, I am lost in reimagining. I lean back and glide on my snowshoes, passing through a forest that I will spend my life trying to understand and to make just a little more alive. There is so much to be done, so many things to be learned and unlearned and remembered. I wish not for a perfect relationship with this forest but for a good one; that we may both become a small piece of a better world.

2 | RESPONSIBILITY: AN IMPERFECT FOREST

My tires press the rusted cable into the sod. I drive past the "Keep Out" sign, bleached and bent and stippled with bullet holes, and up the hill.

The road is faint and overgrown, a steep, narrow path through the woods. As I creep the truck upward, a ravine cuts a jagged scar through the road's center. I straddle it with my tires, bumping and spinning over loose gravel and rounded stones, banking upward. Finally, the road turns to the north and levels, opening into a clearing tufted with yellow grass.

May in Vermont is both spring and summer—a time of hopefulness and promise, a becoming time. As I step out of the truck, the air is warm and humid. The buds of the trees are swollen with expectation, but the light still slices through their bare branches, white and clear. The understory of the forest on the mountain glows faintly green, the soil saturated and awakening.

Logging trash hunches on the margins of the clearing: snarls of rusty skidder cables, crumpled hydraulic fluid buckets, beer cans and bottles, piles of cracked tires, the curling track of an excavator capped with emerald moss. To the north of the clearing is the remnant of a forest, a long plateau of stunted trees leaning in the memories of shadows, oak and pine stumps rotting at their feet. To the west is a kind of wetland, a morass of black ruts filled with murky water. To the south, the clearing opens toward Camels Hump: *Tawapodiiwajo*, the "sitting-place mountain," its summit still crested with frost.

I pull on my canvas vest, its familiar weight settling on my shoulders. I still remember the pride and excitement I felt when I first put on the orange vest, stepping into the uniform of the foresters that I idolized and admired. I remember how strong and heavy it felt, the clean smell of the new cloth. This morning, my vest is as complex and as ornamented as an ancient tree. My compass, my prism, my GPS, my permanent marker are tied on like epiphytes, the once-bright fabric frayed and sun-bleached and speckled with blue paint. My dream of being a forester has become real, as close to me as skin.

This morning I awoke in my apartment by the laundromat and the blinking light of the bodega. The city streets were quiet as I drove past the cemetery and the nursing home, the subsidized housing, the people curled on street corners, the trash gathered in dusty windrows, the raccoons and skunks toddling from hedgerow to the backyard in the half-light. I passed the shopping center and the condominiums, the cul-de-sacs with indigenous names etched onto the memory of a sand plain forest, where little fires once smoldered in the understory.

As the sun reached above the Green Mountains, I drove through the broad valley. I passed through forests that had been cleared, exploited, and degraded, along streams that had been ditched and dammed, straightened and polluted, through ecosystems echoing with the trail of destruction blazed by my ancestors as they walked indelibly and unforgivingly down the road of "progress." I drove through the mists of the *Anthropocene*: the geologic epoch in which humans are the dominant influence on this planet, its climate, its ecosystems, its species. I drove through forests that were both human and wild, both ancient and new.

I scan the battered clearing, sweat tickling the surface of my skin. I feel a kinship with forests like this. Like them, I am many things at once, a creature of divergent worlds—with one foot in the city and another in the woods. As streetlights cast lemony circles on the pavement, I ride my rusted bike to the co-op, to the big communal houses, to the bar. I play electric guitar in a punk band, screaming along with the choruses. I am young and joyful and hopeful and free. Each day at dawn, I wash the glitter of my city life off my face and transform, becoming a forester again. I feel the vest on my shoulders, the worn boots on my feet, and know that, whatever I am, I am also this.

I scan my map, watching the early light glint off the crushed door of a skidder, partially buried in the earth. The photographs on the realtor's website showed only this landing with its panoramic view, mentioning the 175-acre forest as an afterthought. Aerial photos showed a mountain marbled with skid trails, a sign of recent, aggressive logging. The lines on the topographic map crowded together like the growth rings of an ancient tree, suggesting steep, unforgiving terrain. Though nothing about this land seemed promising, I have allowed myself the luxury of hope—the chance to discover something vital and secret in a foreboding world.

A red-tailed hawk cuts across the blue sky, soaring toward the distant ripple of Gleason Brook. I turn toward the sun and follow a skid trail banking unselfconsciously upward. The chipping sparrows chatter at me as I enter a broken forest.

I pause, gulping the thick air. To the west, the cliffs of Stimson Mountain shine through the trees. To the east, Bone Mountain rises, tufted with dark spruce. Between the twin peaks, Joiner Brook crashes through the teeth of the mountains, filling its narrow valley with white noise. My legs burn, my shirt already sticking to my chest. Everywhere the land rises and falls around me, too steep to climb or to descend. Ahead, the skid trail feathers fearlessly upward, clinging to the edge of the slope. There is nowhere to go but up, and so I begin to ascend again.

As I walk, a missing feeling tags my mind, bothering me. I have walked many forests just like this one, sprawled across south-facing slopes in the flinty soils of this Winooski River Valley. These forests are the province of red and white oak, of American beech, of red maple, of red spruce and hemlock—the trees of dry, warm, hard places. This forest is different. I sense that it is somehow incomplete, as shallow and as transparent as a ghost.

The sun casts crooked shadows on the forest floor. On the shoulders of the slope, beech trees curl like tongues, their bark cracked and pockmarked. American beech is a fascinating tree; shade-tolerant and long-lived, patience and persistence embodied. In the forest, it plays the tortoise to the proverbial hare: waiting in the understory for faster-growing, shorter-lived trees to decline and die, subsisting on dapples of sunlight or no direct sunlight at all. When their chance finally comes, beech trees ascend into the canopy with an air of inevitability, where they can tower for four hundred years or more. Two hundred and fifty years ago, 40–60 percent of the trees in this forest were beech, their trunks massive, their bark as silky and as gray as the skin of an elephant. Today, beech haunts the mountain, rattling its windows, trapped in a space between.

The beech trees by the sides of the trail bear little resemblance to the trees that once ruled this mountain: they are small and contorted, their bark broken by countless black lesions. Like nearly all the beech trees that I see, they are suffering from beech bark disease, a nonnative pathogen introduced to North America in the 1920s. Beech bark disease, the combination of a fungus and a scale insect, attacks beech's most distinctive, most personal attribute—its smooth, striking bark—turning it into a moonscape of black cobbles. As it does so, it strikes the heart of beech's evolutionary identity: its longevity, its persistence. Instead of living for four centuries, most beech trees now die in four to six decades. Once an elder that outlasted all the others, beech has become a short-lived species, doomed to suffer and to fail.

I try to imagine a forest of healthy beech: the way the light would have shone against their smooth bark on a spring day like this, how they would have stood like silvery columns, their trunks winking with branch scars like elephant eyes. I imagine, over the millennia, how many bears sat high in the canopy of ancient beech trees on languid autumn afternoons, filling their bellies with beechnuts. I imagine what a forest of healthy beech would have meant to the squirrels and the chipmunks, the turkey and the deer, the birds of the canopy and the fungi of the soil. I imagine how healthy beech trees would have enriched the forest on the mountain, how many worlds they would have held in their arms.

Though beech persists in Vermont's forests, many of the functions and habitats associated with it have vanished—a phenomenon known as *cryptic function loss*. It is not alone. The elms that once towered in the valley bottoms now die from Dutch elm disease in their infancy. The butternuts, planted by Indigenous people for millennia and by colonists for centuries, fade away from butternut canker. The American chestnut, once as common as beech in Appalachian forests, has been virtually erased from this continent by chestnut blight. The ash trees, still standing hopefully on the mountain, will soon be lost to the emerald ash borer. Each of these tree species is unique, each coevolved with each other and with countless other species. Each has stood on the mountain for thousands of years, and each has been lost, or functionally lost, in a matter of decades.

I turn off the skid trail, fighting through a city of finger-sized beech saplings. Beech trees are adept at producing clones from their root systems—especially when stressed—an ingenious adaptation that allows them to prolong their lives indefinitely. Around me, beech sprouts huddle around their parent tree, little more than a shell of broken bark. The clones are as self-assured as children with an impossible dream; ready to live, to become giants, to shower the world with beechnuts. They do not yet understand that their identity has been taken from them, that they inhabit a warped, partial reality. I wrap my fingers around a sapling, its slender trunk already cracked and rough. The beech clones are doomed to suffer the same fate as their parents: to decline and to die, to produce clones that will carry the same futile dream into the future. The cycle repeats itself, again and again: a species, once foundational to the health and vibrance of this forest, caught in a loop.

As the beech trees on the mountain breach endless waves of mortality, as they sprout and sprout, their clones crowd out the oak and the maple, the yellow birch, the spruce. Across generations of growth and decline, they form a monoculture in the forest's understory—an impenetrable mass of a species that will never be healthy and that will also not allow anything else to exist. Beech bark disease has transformed beech from a pillar into a pest, from a foundational part of this forest community into a species that stands between this forest and its diversity, its health, its resilience.

I sigh. Like the beech sprouts, I am hopeful and hopeless, an orphan of the Anthropocene. Like the beech sprouts, I was born into a world of extinction and invasion, degradation and deforestation, fragmentation and loss. Like the beech sprouts, I know only the aftermath: a landscape of disconnection and uncertainty, a world of drought and famine and disaster, a changing climate and ecosystems on the run. In my young life, I have never known a forest of healthy beech, chestnut, elm, or butternut, can only imagine what they may once have been. I have only ever known beech as a nuisance, a barrier between a forest and its vitality. In forests in which beech was once an anchor, I know it only as a pest.

I fight through the understory, coppery beech leaves sliding under my feet. This forest, like this world, is a strange gift: a promise of abundance now cracked and twisted and riddled with sores. It is filtered through the legacies of the past and the realities of the present. By the time it reaches my eye, something has been lost.

The wandering song of a winter wren travels across the still air. The songbirds are returning, bustling and fussing through the naked canopies of the trees. As they always have, they are preparing to nest, to raise broods of chicks, to live their bursting summer lives. I lean against a bigtooth aspen, its gangly trunk swaying over the beech sea, listening to the saccharine trills of a golden-crowned kinglet.

There is more to this story. I wander west, over slopes and ridges, through narrow valleys and across dripping seeps. I walk for another half-hour before I realize that every tree of every species is struggling, limping along, dying. In a flash, I remember the aerial photo, the logging roads splitting the forest like white watersheds. I blink and suddenly I see the signs: the stumps and the treetops, rotting in the leaves.

I travel back in time. Thirty years ago, the air in this forest was sharp with the fermented tang of cut oak. I can see the sugar maple stumps bleeding sweetly into piles of shavings, the yellow birch stumps frosted with orange, minty sap, the oak stumps still red and hard and flat. This forest was high-graded: an unethical and short-sighted type of timber harvesting in which all the healthiest and most valuable trees are cut and the less healthy and less valuable are left behind. This forest was treated like a mine, its value extracted without any thought for its future.

A cool breeze carries me back to the present. I look up through the canopy of dying beech, their bodies contorted and stunted, their branches tipped with dead wood like fingers of ivory. Thirty years ago, these beech trees were waiting in the dappled shade. As the loggers cut the oaks and the maples and the yellow birches, they passed the beech trees by. As the oily smell of diesel exhaust faded from this forest, the beech trees were suddenly liberated, with nothing but the blue sky to conquer. Like aging starlets, they prepared to press back the velvet curtains, to rebuild the forest of beech on the mountain. Only then, as they reached upward, did they realize that they had become something else, that they would never be themselves again.

In front of me, beech trees crowd around an oak stump, its edges rounded and softened by time. The beeches are witches at a caldron, leaning inward, their bodies decorated with wooly clusters of scale, skirted by a growing mass of clones. Around them is a dystopian forest: everywhere I look, beeches are dying, white birch trees declining, aspen disintegrating, red maples at the edge of their lives. A monoculture of diseased beech saplings presses through the understory, fated to inherit the forest of the future.

As the birds run their cheerful errands through the canopy, the forest is the memory of something beautiful, withering like cut flowers. Like all the forests of my life, it echoes with trauma, defined by centuries of exploitation and mismanagement, by a climate crisis and a biodiversity crisis, a mass extinction, by non-native plants, pests, and pathogens, by a society that values forests only for the pieces of them that can be sold. I want to believe that this forest has a future, but I cannot see it.

A little brook tumbles downward, diving over boulders laced with blue lichen. I descend, my eyes on my feet. Once, this was a stand of hemlock, a shaded and secret place, home to deer and bear and porcupines. Now, it is a field of jumbled rock and moss-covered stumps, the soil between them washed away. I slide and trip downward, catching myself on the slim trunks of mountain maples. When I look up, I have entered a different world.

A tall, gray cliff towers over me. In its shadow is a young forest: red maple, white birch, and white pine trees standing like soldiers, their trunks uniform and straight. The earth, stretched severely over the rocks above, feels cool and dark and deep. Down the hill, the white light of a utility corridor slices through the shade of the forest, transmission lines sagging from east to west. Distantly, I see the silver slash of the highway, cars and trucks flickering through the trees. Engines drone over the gentle sounds of the spring forest.

Three centuries ago, European colonists surged into North America, spilling into an endless wilderness. The "New World" they conquered was already ancient, already home to cultures as rich and as complex as their own—neither new nor open nor free. Across this continent, Europeans moved into coastal settlements littered with human bones, pastured cattle in fields created by millennia of Indigenous burning, plowed soils formed in the kettles of wetlands from which the last beaver was trapped a century before.

To these colonists, New England's forests seemed inexhaustible, and they took from them with reckless abandon. They cut trees for firewood—before the advent of the woodstove, an average home might use dozens of cords per year—for fences, for houses and barns, for smelting iron, for lime kilns, for boiling maple sap into syrup. By the mid-1800s, hundreds of thousands of acres of timber and millions of cords of wood were needed annually to supply the railroad industry alone.

What was a trickle in the 1700s became a flood. Colonists rushed up the broad valleys and down the long lake, into New England and beyond. Merino sheep were brought to Vermont in 1811, and by 1837 there were between 1 million and 1.7 million

42

sheep in Vermont and around 4 million in New England. By 1850, 60–80 percent of New England had been cleared over the span of a single generation, much of it for sheep pasture.

Through the straight trees of the young forest, a *wolf tree*—a tree that stood like a lone wolf in the middle of a field for a century or more—looms. Like many of Vermont's wolf trees, this one is a sugar maple, its trunk massive and hollow and twisted, its branches reaching into the memory of the endless pasture. Centuries old, the wolf tree is dying, walking near the end of a long path. It has nothing left to prove and so sinks contentedly into the young forest on the mountain, like a grandparent surrounded by grandchildren.

I approach the wolf tree, laying a hand on its furrowed bark. The tree is an overripe peach, a veneer of living flesh wrapped around a column of crumbling wood. Cavities speckle its trunk and its branches, their thresholds scratched by beaks and teeth and claws. I touch a garden of mosses and lichens on its trunk, a forest in miniature. Moisture leaks from a knothole far above, and in the forest under my fingers it is raining.

Once, an ancient forest covered this mountain. When the first European colonists came to this place, this forest was a living city thousands of years in the making, a community built of legacy and continuity, resilience and adaptability, time and change. Over just decades the ancient city was disassembled, its history undone, its identity lost to a field of green grass, baking in the sun. Today, all that remains is the wolf tree, its yellowed pages fluttering.

I watch the light travel through the wolf tree's broken crown, listening to the roar of the highway. Sixty years ago, the interstate drew a straight line through this broad valley, rolling from west to east. The highway was uncompromising and unsentimental, slicing through houses and dooryards, pastures and hayfields, calving farmhouses from their farmland. From where I stand, I can see an old farmhouse and barn on the far side of its rushing lanes, the place that the sheep and then the cows that grazed this hillside called home for 150 years. The interstate and this forest are siblings, connected in time: as the first cars sped down the highway, the people who drove sheep and cattle up this hill for generations looked across the silver divide, their land suddenly distant from them. As they watched, their pasture roughened, tiny trees simmering in the sod. After one and a half centuries in exile, the forest returned to the mountain.

While forests now cover about 75 percent of Vermont, they are not the same as those that were cleared centuries ago. On this spring day, the young forest under the cliffs seems as thin and as transparent as paper, as different from the ancient forest as its straight young trees are from the wolf tree. Connections have yet to be drawn, soils yet to be deepened, richness and complexity yet to be rediscovered. Like the beech trees above, the young forest is an example of cryptic function loss: while it persists, many of the functions, the characteristics, and the habitats that once defined it are missing.

Though I am young, I know that I will not live to see this forest become ancient again. In a few weeks, the trees of the young forest will open their leaves into another growing season, will reach twigs and branches outward and upward, will expand themselves in tiny measures. At the end of each growing season, they will be a quarter-inch wider, a handspan taller. I lean on the blue-gray bark of a red maple, watching the cars on the highway pass by. As the children in these cars age, as they parent children, as their children have children of their own, this forest will still be young.

Above me, the wind combs the treetops. I scan the cliffs, the young forest, the power lines, the rushing highway. This is the world that I know: a world of beauty and promise and edges, of wildness bounded like lightning in a bottle. These are the forests I know: monuments to colonization and exploitation and an unimaginable but finite resilience.

Like me, this forest is doing its best, building a life in the world it has been offered. As I dream of what my life may become, we are both at the beginning of a long journey, both seedlings planted in the ashes of an uncompromising past. We are what we are.

A truck on the highway grinds its gears. I bend to look at a sugar maple seedling, its tiny buds just beginning to swell. I grasp its little trunk between my fingers, thinking how strange it is that every massive tree must first endure the indignity of being no bigger than a dandelion, small enough to be girdled by a vole, nibbled by a rabbit, crushed by a fawn's delicate cloven hoof. This maple may one day be a giant, but today it is as vulnerable as a lamb in the grass.

The 1800s marked a moment in what historian Frank Graham called the "Age of Extermination." The wildlife of North America faded to the margins, their habitats destroyed, hunted for fur, food, and sport, predators exterminated out of a perverse sense of duty. In Vermont, caribou, moose, and elk, once the dominant herbivores on this landscape, disappeared by the late 1700s. Their predators—wolves and the eastern cougar— soon followed. Across the eighteenth and nineteenth centuries, many other species, including deer, beaver, fisher, marten, otter, bear, turkeys, and Canada geese were extirpated from Vermont, or had populations so low that they were undetectable.

By the beginning of the twentieth century, wildlife populations across North America, from forest to prairie, had been changed forever. The herds of hundreds of millions of buffalo, the flocks of billions of passenger pigeons, the beaver dams that once filled Vermont's valleys at densities of hundreds per square mile, the salmon rushing fin to fin, the bands of gangly wolves: all had become myths, stories of a lost past.

Some wildlife species—beaver, fisher (sometimes known as fisher cat), turkey, and white-tailed deer—were reintroduced into Vermont in the late 1800s and early 1900s. Others, like otters, bears, and Canada geese, returned naturally. Others remain missing. Like the loss or the functional loss of a tree species, the ripples created by the loss of a wildlife species are unknowable. Each of this forest's species is unique, the product of eons of evolution, an answer to the earth's many enigmatic questions. Each is a member of a natural community, an intricate web of connections and relationships. Each is precious. As I kneel on the hillside, the Age of Extermination continues: global animal populations have declined an average of 68 percent since 1970. Some 680 species of vertebrate animals, along with perhaps one hundred thousand species of invertebrates, have gone extinct since the 1600s. One million others are threatened with extinction.

I look past the little sugar maple, across the contours of the slope. The coals of the future smolder in the young forest's understory, a carpet of tiny oak and ash and sugar maple seedlings. The forest of tomorrow is already here, waiting for a chance to reach into the canopy. It will not come. The seedlings are contorted and strange, their short trunks twisting and changing direction. Their promised stature a distant dream, the seedlings' buds and twigs have been browsed by deer, again and again.

Today, white-tailed deer—once a stranger to this mountain—are this forest's primary large herbivores, and coyotes, a species endemic to central and southwestern North America (first seen in Vermont in the 1940s), are its primary large predators. White-tailed deer are generalists and opportunists, ideally suited to this fragmented and developed world. With their predators and their competitors gone, deer have thrived in this modern landscape, becoming overpopulated in much of the United States. Through the subtle act of browsing tree buds and twigs, deer can fundamentally change the shape, the substance, and the future of a forest, causing certain species of trees or plants to disappear and favoring others. As innocuous as this may seem, it is not: today, deer overpopulations are considered one of the most serious threats to the health of ecosystems, and the species that rely on them, across much of this country.

In this young forest, my instincts tell me that the sugar maples should be pushing upward through the understory, ascending toward the canopy. Instead, tree species that deer avoid browsing—beech, hop hornbeam, witch hazel, striped maple—dominate, casting the sugar maple seedlings in low shade. As they have done across North America, deer have taken charge of this forest; they have decided what species of trees will thrive here, what this forest will become. Because of the deer, these sugar maple seedlings will never become wolf trees, will never bloom forests of lichen from their craggy bark, will never build root systems that plumb the cracks in the mountain. Because of the deer, the habitats and natural processes unique to sugar maple will be absent from the forest of the future. I watch the carpet of seedlings, stunted and without hope, wondering what this forest will become.

Ecosystems are a balancing act, both resilient and sensitive. A species that is a normal and even beneficial part of forest ecology—like deer, like beech—can become a biodiversity threat when confronted with the loss of a predator, a dramatic change in habitat, a nonnative pathogen, or a change in environmental conditions. In this moment, the beech on the mountain suffers, while the deer on the mountain thrive. Both are threats to the integrity of this forest.

The power lines hum. I think of my home in the city; the rats and the skunks in the alleys, the European house sparrows and pigeons and starlings roosting on asphalt shingles. I look across the stunted seedlings in the young forest's understory, the trees whose future has been taken from them. I am a member of a generation like these seedlings: we reach for the sun, promised freedom and opportunity, every grand and beautiful thing. The world beckons, offering us the chance to become ancient, powerful, and prominent, a generation of towering trees, the forest of the future. As we grow, we are beset by challenges and threats, stunted by a world that rattles with broken promises, a world that offers everything to some and nothing to others. We are vulnerable and tender, twisted and strange. We fight to survive, to find purpose and meaning, to find ourselves and each other. The changed world drags us down.

The highway roars in my ears. This forest is an unsettling dream, a landscape of familiar things arranged in a way that makes no sense. I feel a gaping dissonance, the distance between what this forest should be and what it has become.

A queen bumblebee buzzes by me, the fuzzy little bear of the insect world. I turn and follow her eastward across the slope. Each spring, queen bumblebees emerge from their burrows in the leaves, regal and solitary, to build their colonies and their lives anew. They are not truly alone: somewhere, Dutchman's breeches and squirrel corn—the *Dicentra* sisters—hang their enigmatic flowers, waiting for the queen to carry their pollen across the mountain. My heart lifts, hoping that the bumblebee will lead me to a garden of *Dicentra*.

But when I crest a narrow ridge, I stop, inhaling sharply. Below me, Japanese barberry fills the forest like green smoke. Barberry is one of many nonnative invasive plants, animals, pests, and pathogens that have colonized our ecosystems, one of many introduced species that undermine forests' health and their habitat and their function, which pose another major threat to global biodiversity.

Somewhere, Japanese barberry is a part of a native ecosystem, vital and precious, serving a valuable ecological role. Yet here, in this forest—free of the pests, predators, competitors, and environmental limitations that it has coevolved with for thousands of years—it displaces native species, derails natural processes, and erodes the vitality and resilience of this forest.

I rest my hands on my hips. In the decades to come, wind-storms and ice storms will sweep across the mountain. Trees will live and grow and die here, and the forest will reach toward diversity, toward legacy and continuity, toward resilience, toward the attributes that once defined the ancient forests. As it has for millennia, change will call to this forest, offering it the opportunity to regenerate, to deepen itself, to build itself anew. This time, the forest will not answer. With every gap opened in the canopy, the barberry will spread, tighten its grip, smother the seedlings and the plants of the understory. The more the forest changes, the more the barberry will spread. With each passing year, the forest will slide farther into dysfunction, its tires spinning deeper and deeper into the mud.

In an alien and alienated world, our leaves flutter, the stems of barberry closing around us. The members of my community experience addiction and mental health disorders, encounter racism and inequity, are unable to access economic opportunity, are unable to protect this planet and each other. We live in a forest of our grandparents' choices: a changing climate, unjust institutions, a broken, bleeding world. Like this forest, we march like ants toward a future that serves no one, impossible and inevitable.

I descend into the barberry patch, feeling unanchored and adrift. I feel an odd kinship with this forest, this island of misfit toys. I am also battered and broken, looking at the forest through half a lens. My generation and I are also children of this Anthropocene, this biosphere of broken promises. Like this forest, we are creatures of legacy, the wounds of the past echoing through us.

I know that even as this forest reels from the legacies of the past, even as it navigates an untenable present, an unknown future opens before it. In the years and decades to come, there will be new pests and pathogens, a climate changing faster than ever, more species fading and blinking out of existence. Even as this forest searches for what it has lost, the hill it must climb grows higher each day.

The barberry thorns claw at me as I move across the hillside. I know that this forest is beyond inaction, that it will not save itself, and I wonder: If I do not help this forest, who will? If it is even possible, it would take a lifetime to bring this ecosystem back from the brink of collapse. If it is even possible, it would be an act of immense dedication and an act of faith, potentially futile.

A brown creeper sings above the white noise of the highway. An airplane patters overhead. My phone thrums in my pocket. I am lost in a world that is everything and nothing at once.

I turn away, stumbling around ledges and house-sized boulders. I cross places where sheep once huddled as spring rains washed the naked body of the earth, across gullies that crack the lips of the mountain, its soils gently eroding away. I trace the base of the cliffs, searching for a path upward. Finally, I see a deer trail angling through a narrow pass in the rock. I crest the cliffs and am greeted by crowd of diseased beech, dying in the spring light. To the north, a light flashes through the trees—my truck, baking in the sun.

I start the truck and sit with my eyes closed, letting the cool air roll over me. I feel the pull of hopelessness, the drumming despair, the loneliness of living in this broken world. For a moment, I let the feeling draw me down, pulling me below the surface of its dark waters.

When I open my eyes, the sun is slanting through the bare trees, tacking toward *hitawbagw*—"the lake between"—and the Adirondacks beyond. The slopes on the far side of the valley are a rainbow of muted colors, billions of tiny buds in their reds and yellows and greens waiting to open into the humid air. Beneath the waking trees, black bears wallow in muddy seeps. Tom turkeys gobble and strut as hens pick and cluck around them. Woodcocks bob and dance, their wings whistling at dusk. Spring blooms, inviting everything to become itself again.

It is all too much. I shift the truck into gear, steering down the gravel road, across the bleeding ravine, past the "Keep Out" sign and over the rusted cable. I follow the paved road through the little village of Bolton Flats and west through the floodplains of the big river, joining the highway in Richmond. As the on-ramp swings me around, it shows me the towering ridge of Mount Mansfield, the altar of Camels Hump, two ancient sisters still frosted with snow. The Winooski River splits the world between them, pulling the waters of the broad valley into its green body. For a moment I see the broken ridgeline of Stimson Mountain, its south face crumbling. Then, it is gone.

I put miles between myself and the forest on the mountain. The highway carries me through forests fragmented by driveways and houses, clearcut for strip malls and box stores, through housing developments named after the animals and the trees they displaced. I speed toward the city on the shore of the long lake, where music pulses from the rooftops and screens flash through open windows.

I think of my species, the billions of people living at the grace of a finite planet spinning through cavernous space. We have arisen from ecosystems to become a force as primal and earth-shaking as a glacier, shaping this planet physically, biologically, chemically, climatically. We have sent the biosphere that sustains us into a profound reorganization. We teeter on an unsteady foundation, moving into an uncertain future together.

Though we have the power to protect these ecosystems and species, to save this biosphere and to save ourselves in the process, we do not. We continue to transform forests, to undermine them, to degrade them each day. We are trapped in a whirlpool of inertia and tradition, trapped inside institutions built for an infinite and imaginary world. As our influence ripples through every ecosystem on earth, those of us who love ecosystems imagine that it is a kindness to leave the remaining pieces of this biosphere alone: to do nothing to help them heal. Only we, the modern humans, would have the arrogance to ask such a thing from our ecosystems.

The radio chatters about ecosystems dying, species going extinct, scientists' increasingly panicked and dire warnings. Soon the buds of the beech trees on Stimson Mountain will open, their bodies rippling with disease. The deer will wind across the hillside, nipping the buds of sugar maple and oak. Barberry will spread through the understory, choking out the *Dicentra*.

I mourn the forest on the mountain and also my own courage—that I am not brave enough to try to save it. It is just one of countless forests, a tiny piece of this tilting reality. I am just one of billions of people who abdicate my responsibility for the world that we have created, for the choices of our ancestors, for the lives of future generations.

I wallow in my grief, reaching for water that flowed through my grandparents' fingers long ago. I turn the radio up and speed down the shining highway, putting the forest on the skirts of Stimson Mountain out of my mind.

Spring has become summer. I drive east through the broad valley, passing through a living world that feels bright and lush and full of promise. As I through turn onto the overgrown road, the "Keep Out" sign is invisible, obscured by layers of green life. The forest around me is a wall of green, new leaves filling every space. I steer the truck upward, my tires finally settling in the tall grass of the landing.

Over the last month, as this forest awakened into summer, my despair and my anger have softened. I have dreamed out loud to my friends and family, describing the forest on the mountain with a growing tenderness. I have craned my neck toward the cliffs of Stimson Mountain as I rode the flats of the highway, searching it with my eyes. I have read about restoring degraded forests, about how we might use our power to help forests like this become whole again. Where I once felt only emptiness, I have let myself kindle an ember of hope.

I walk up the steep trail, the forest around me bubbling with life. Ravens *qwark* from the pines, squirrels skittering through the leaves. The wandering tracks of a black bear meander ahead of me, crossed by turkeys and foxes and the tiny prints of scores of racing chipmunks. The forest's understory has become a field of lowbush blueberries, their flowers like white bells. The air is filled with the buzzing of insects and the songs of warblers and wrens and thrushes.

The fullness of summer envelops the mountain. The forest is a centuries-old house, its doors hanging on their hinges, its windows milky and broken. Birds flit across the hanging eaves, weaving tiny round nests with dried grasses and slivers of birch bark, a ribbon from a balloon, a thread of blue tarp. Coyotes hunt house mice in its flaking halls, tadpoles wriggling under clapboards bearded with sheaves of dripping moss. The forest sags under the weight of an unkind past, an impossible present, an unknown future, and still it clings to its beauty.

The forest inside of me is changing. I am turning from spring to summer, breaking bud, growing up. I am beginning to realize that this world belongs to us now, whoever and whatever we are. I am beginning to realize that only we can fulfill our promises to this biosphere, to this forest, to future generations. I am ready to step into responsibility, to live a life of purpose, to help build a better world. Like this forest, I am crooked and imperfect. Like this forest, I am called toward wholeness.

The light on the mountain has changed. While I still see the wounds that riddle the body of this forest, I now find sparks of hope and beauty. I discover tall cliffs and clear, tumbling streams. I find a few smooth-barked beech trees, their trunks patterned by the claws of generations of black bears. I find serviceberry and sweet fern, Corydalis and columbine, a few reclusive ginseng. I find overlooks capped in reindeer moss and bobcat lays etched into the rocks. I see a forest fighting to discover itself inside of this moment. I know the feeling.

I push through a beech thicket, finding myself on a dome of rock overlooking the broad valley. I think of my friends, my band, my little community in the city. Even as the world around us contracts, even as we struggle under the weight of institutions that do not serve us, even as we confront unjust and harmful legacies left for us by past generations, we are rediscovering what it means to live in this world—what it means to take care of ourselves, what it means to take care of each other. In spite of everything, we are searching roots, reaching for freedom, happiness and purpose, winding toward sweetness in the dark. Despite everything, we believe that our destiny, and the destiny of this world, is not to be broken but to be beautiful.

A red-tailed hawk wings through the valley, rising toward the glowing mountains. High above me, its eyes are black pearls, looking over a landscape that is forever changed and forever changing. I stand, my hands open, responsibility ringing through me.

3 | LEGACY: BIOGRAPHY OF A WOLF TREE

Once upon a time, as the mountain awakened to the promise of spring, a sugar maple opened its scaled buds, reaching into an upturned world.

The sugar maple was a member of a biological community of diversity and depth, an ancient forest built of thousands of years of adaptation and change. Now, the ancient forest was gone, its trees remembered only by their stumps. The sugar maple was an island in an open ocean, standing nakedly in a field of broken earth. Around it, leaning pyres dotted the slope, centuries of dead wood waiting to be burned. White sheep wandered the mountain's once-secret hollows, grazing tufts of yellow grass. Only the sugar maple remained.

Despite everything, the sugar maple bloomed, decorating its branches with flowers like green bells. Despite everything, the sugar maple's male flowers sent tiny grains of pollen floating into the *aeolian plankton*: the world of tiny things that drift in the wind. Despite everything, the sugar maple waited, its female flowers bobbing, arrayed in a posture of hope.

Somewhere to the east was another survivor, another sugar maple tree that had weathered the apocalypse of deforestation, another tree that had dared to flower in this new world. Somehow, a grain of its pollen landed on one of the sugar maple's female flowers: settling delicately onto the tender stigma, pulled down into the secret chamber of the ovary.

Weeks passed. The sugar maple's flowers withered as its crown filled with broad, perfect leaves. As robins built nests in the sugar maple's branches and filled them with speckled blue eggs, the ovary subtly swelled. As the robins fed their naked, chirping chicks, *samaras*—tiny oval seeds adorned with long green wings, dangling in delicate, waiting pairs—began to take shape.

Gathered inside one of the samaras was an impossible dream: a tree fated to stand like a lone wolf on the mountain, an island of wildness in a barren sea.

Spring became summer. As the wolf tree expanded inside its seed, the world around it was both ancient and new. For hundreds of thousands of years, the broad valley had changed: glaciers expanding and retreating, living worlds chased southward and pulled northward again and again over unthinkable eons of time. All the while, tides of species had come and gone from the broad valley, adapting and evolving, combining and recombining, forming communities built of relationship and resilience, legacy and change.

The first people had lived in the broad valley for hundreds of generations. For thousands of years, they had traveled the big river as it meandered through floodplains alive with beaver wetlands and glittering oxbow ponds. For thousands of years, they had hunted in forests of beech and butternut, elm and chestnut, forests they shared with elk and wolves and cougars, with the beavers that dammed the river and the passenger pigeons that darkened the skies.

The first people were members of the species *Homo sapiens*: a species that, like all others, had been formed in the womb of the biosphere, their bodies and their behaviors carrying the legacies of a million-year journey through time. Though their origin was common, humans had become unique, emergent, unlike the others. Though they were small and soft, unprotected by claws and scales, they were able to thrive in and dominate nearly every ecosystem on earth. Everywhere that they went, they changed the world.

As the samara ripened on the sugar maple, the first people had been decimated by disease, murdered and displaced, their land and their culture taken from them, their ancestral forests stolen and replaced by a world of pastures, baking in the sun. The creatures with which they shared thousands of years of history— the beavers, the bears, the deer, the Canada geese, the turkeys, the marten and the fisher, the elk and the caribou, the wolves and the cougars—had been lost from the broad valley and the valleys beyond.

The samara hardened, its stalk becoming brown and brittle. One morning, a late-summer wind brushed the sugar maple's leaves, breaking the samara's slender tether and sending it spinning into the open air. For a moment the samara was a bird on the wing, spiraling over fields dotted with sheep, over naked hills segmented by arrow-straight fences. As it flew outward and downward, the new people of the valley were in the fields, reaping hay and grain, picking potatoes. The mountain was naked and golden, brown water carving sinuous gullies in its slopes.

The white bodies of the new people were also a product of the biosphere, a legacy of the evolutionary journey that they had taken together with the first people of the valley. For millions of years the first people and the new people had walked together, as a single people. Though their paths had diverged for just a few millennia, just a brief moment in an endless span of time, they had become different things. Like the first people, the new people of the valley sustained themselves on the riches of ecosystems. Unlike the first people, the new people viewed the ecosystems of the valley as things to be conquered and subjugated, mined for personal wealth. Unlike the first people, they cleared the ancient forests, drained the wetlands, straightened the rivers, hunted the wildlife to extinction.

As powerful as the new people felt, they were as delicate and as vulnerable as the wolf tree's samara, carried on the wind. The new people lived at the grace of the very ecosystems that they destroyed, breathing its air and drinking its water. As they farmed the rich soils of the valley, their crops were pollinated by wild insects, sustained by the communities of the living soil, watered by clouds seeded by trees. Even as they marveled at their own power, the new people balanced on a razor's edge: vulnerable to the slightest variations in season or temperature, drought or precipitation, to a climate always a hair's breadth away from uninhabitable. They were the earth's strangest children, chipping away at the foundation of a biosphere that offered them life.

The wolf tree's samara alighted on the scarred turf of a rocky pasture, its journey coming to an end. Rains came, and the samara sank into the sod. The days shortened and soon the mountain was covered in white. Field mice scurried over the samara in their tunnels beneath the snow.

The earth softened, becoming warm and pregnant with water. The samara sprouted, a tiny root searching downward, a green stalk rising like a delicate periscope into the sunlight. Soon, a pair of ornate leaves announced the wolf tree's identity to the world: sugar maple, *senomoziak*, the sugar tree.

As the mountain strained to become forest again, sheep meandered across its slopes, their wooly heads bent, clipping young trees and shrubs with their yellow teeth. As a seedling in the pasture ocean, the wolf tree was bumped and jostled, stepped on by the sheep, and gnawed by voles. Somehow, it survived. Over years of summers, the wolf tree became a sapling with a slender trunk and branches of its own.

One day, the new people, the temperamental gods of the valley, approached the wolf tree as they cleared brush from the mountainside pasture. With axes hanging at their sides, they touched its rough bark, smiled gently, and walked away. The wolf tree had their blessing.

The wolf tree grew up an orphan, a stranger to the twisted oaks of the cliffs and the soaring elms of the valley bottoms. With no trees to compete with, it stretched its limbs outward like a child in an oversized bed, building a rich, full, globe of a crown, a thick, plated trunk, a wide, sinking root system. In summer, the sheep gathered in the wolf tree's shade, sleeping between the sloping buttresses of its roots.

Decades passed on the mountain. The sheep were replaced by cows, and the steepest and most remote pastures were abandoned, regenerating into cities of emerald pines. Brown cattle silently and purposefully chewed under the wolf tree's growing canopy, watching the big river flow nakedly through the endless pastures below. Generations had passed since the forests were cleared from the broad valley, and the new people had forgotten what this place had once been. The ancient forest and its creatures were yarns spun by elders at kitchen tables: tall tales, little more than myths.

As the wolf tree expanded from every edge, so too did the communities of the new people. Their roads, their farms, and their homes spread through the floodplains of the big river, clustering at its rapids. The new people were no longer visitors to this place—they had built a complex society in the broad valley, had built lives over and through its contours. Though they had no right to this place, it had become their home.

Like the first people, the new people were bound to the legacies of the past. Each generation was born as soft and as bright as seedlings, spreading roots into a world as ancient and as layered as soil. Along with pastures and roads, rivers and stumps, they inherited institutions and rules, customs, and traditions. They inherited a world in which access to justice, equity, safety, and opportunity depended on where and to whom they were born, on the color and the shape of their bodies. They inherited a world in which some were born into wealth and privilege while others were born into poverty and prejudice and trauma. They could not choose the legacies that they inherited, only what they would make of them: how they would live in the world they had been given.

The sugar maple grew as each generation built their lives atop the legacies of the past—creating legacies that would shape the world of the future.

In 1927 the big river rose, swelling profanely against its banks. The new people had built their lives around the river, had ditched, dammed, and straightened it, had surrounded it with roads, railways, and dams. They had built their houses and farms atop its spreading floodplains, where the earth was flat and the soil was dark and deep.

The new people had misunderstood the river. They had imagined that a river was a volume of water, static and unchanging, a line to be mapped and charted. They did not understand that the river was defined not by stasis but by dynamism—by how it ranged over its flat shoulders, how it broke its banks, how it joyfully and spontaneously reinvented itself. They did not understand that that the valley *was* the river; that the river was an expansive community stretching from foothill to foothill. They did not understand that, like a forest, the nature of a river is to change.

Below the wolf tree, the big river's waters roiled until they became coffee brown. The river had lived a life of exile, separated from its true identity for a century. Now, it joined rivers across the country as they rioted and became themselves again. Everywhere, rivers broke their chains and tore down the bridges, rolled through the brick villages and carried away the cattle. With a rush the big river burst through the railroad dike, spilling over roads and barns, lifting houses off their foundations. Currents swirled through the farmhouse at the base of the mountain, drowning the weathered floorboards and rising up the white plaster. Through the rain, the families of the little village carried their children and drove their livestock up the mountain. Soaked and panting, they huddled under the wolf tree, its roots anchored in the flinty soil, its bare branches swinging in the wind.

The rain finally died. Weeks passed, and the river returned to its channel like a purring lion after a hunt. The wolf tree sprouted leaves as the people of the valley picked through their ruined village, as they rebuilt the road and the railroad, as their houses rose like seedlings from the ashes of a forest fire. The people persisted, their lives changed forever, a legacy of trauma burning in their bodies. They wrapped their pain in heavy cloth, passing it like a dusty heirloom to their children.

In the flood, the big river had reinvented itself—birthing new islands, carving oxbows and meanders. In the remnant forests of the floodplains, the storm had broken and felled trees, had torn gaps in the arching canopy. Tree trunks decorated the forest floor, snags of elm and silver maple standing crookedly above. In the years that followed, a new generation of trees reached upward into the light, each a child of the storm. As the great flood faded into memory, the young trees of the floodplain carried its legacy into the future, manifested in life.

Decades passed, measured in the subtle deepening of the wolf tree's roots, in its thickening trunk, in its expanding crown. The wolf tree's lobed leaves spread and fell in their colors, each year a few more than the last.

In 1962, the twin black tongues of the highway unfurled from east to west, separating the wolf tree's pasture from the farmhouse and the barn in the valley. The lowing cows pressed against the highway fence, four lanes of asphalt dividing them from their rocky pasture on the mountain.

The roar of the highway rattled the windows of the farmhouse. The farmer sat at his kitchen table, his hands spread over an advertisement for a shiny bulk milk tank, a cup of coffee gone cold at its corner. Through his window, he watched as the cattle milled in the muddy barnyard, the barn's red paint flaking, tall milk cans rusting in its shadow. Past the rushing chasm of the highway, the farmer watched the pasture on the mountain roughen with shrubs and young trees. He watched as the legacy of five generations of his family, the legacy of ancestors who broke themselves on the mountain, went fallow.

The farmer placed one hand over the other, a scarred palm resting across a range of bony knuckles. This land had fed him, had built his home, had raised his children. Now it left him as summer left the valley, drifting quietly and inevitably away. Autumn came and the leaves turned their colors. The farmer stared out the window in his patched overalls. The wolf tree stood on the mountain, a beacon of orange flame.

The cows were loaded onto a trailer and hauled away. Each morning the farmer left the farmhouse with a lunch pail swinging at his side, climbed into his pickup truck, and drove to a new job in town. On weekends he busied himself in his dooryard, setting his jaw as the pasture on the mountain became a rainbow of colors, a simple world becoming wild and complex and alive.

Around the wolf tree, the forest returned to the mountain. Somehow, it had been there all along, thrumming as softly as the heartbeat of a hibernating animal. Somehow, in a place that had changed forever, the legacy of something ancient persisted, secret and vital. Now it awoke, spreading from secret places in the earth where a wild world still pulsed.

First came the opportunists: goldenrod and meadowsweet piercing the tufts of yellow grass. Raspberry and blackberry seeds that had lain dormant in the soil for decades sprouted, becoming arching, thorny canes. Next came the trees: the delicate balls of white pine, the crimson twigs of red maple, the pale, racing shoots of aspen. Song sparrows and chipping sparrows sang from the pines. Woodcocks strutted through the brush.

The young trees spread their shy roots downward, tunneling through soil crushed and muddied by the hooves of sheep and cattle for more than a century. Slowly, the soil began to remember itself, to recall that it was a constellation of stone and air, wood and water; a living thing, part vegetable, part animal, part mineral. As the roots of the young trees searched downward, they were bound and infused with the wandering hyphae of mycorrhizal fungi, spreading outward from the wolf tree, its mammoth root system like an open hand. Around the roots of the trees, the rhizosphere rebuilt itself, becoming a metropolis of tiny, critical things, glowing in the dark.

Once, the mountain's forests were ancient. Once, they were defined by legacy and continuity, built atop foundations laid by countless past generations. For millennia, each generation of trees had reached into the next, each leaving biological and ecological legacies rippling in its wake. For millennia, these legacies had made forests diverse and complex, resilient and emergent, vibrant and greater than the sum of their parts.

The trees of the young forest were orphans, still missing the legacies that had defined the ancient forest and its living community. The young forest was built over different kinds of legacies:

growing through fences of barbed wire and rounded stone, over cellar holes and between the rusted gears of farm equipment.

Though it had just begun its life, the young forest was already a survivor, already a miracle of resilience. Somehow, in small measures, the young forest began to rediscover abundance. It began to live again.

After a lifetime spent shading cattle and sheep, the wolf tree became a refuge, sheltering worlds of wild things. Within the young forest, the wolf tree was a *biological legacy*: an elder in a sea of children, fundamentally unlike the young trees on the mountain. As the forest on the mountain began to remember itself, the wolf tree enriched it, offering it something ancient and complex.

As the young trees raced upward, the wolf tree deepened itself, opening into the life-giving miracle of death. As the young trees expanded their crowns, the wolf tree gracefully declined, enacting the decades- or centuries-long perimortem period common to ancient trees. As the young trees built tall, perfect trunks, the wolf tree's trunk hollowed, its wood marbling with rot. As the young trees competed with each other, the ambition that had driven the wolf tree in its youth became acceptance and equanimity.

The wolf tree's bark became shaggier, its fissures deeper. As its trunk was cast into shade, dozens of species of mosses, lichens, and liverworts, some of which took centuries to establish, spread across the wolf tree's body. A city of invertebrates—hundreds of species of moth and butterfly caterpillars, spiders and slugs, mites and springtails—built lives in the cracks and crevices of the wolf tree's bark and brown creepers ranged over its scarred body, foraging in the folds of its gray skin. In summer, bats roosted under shelves of bark on the wolf tree's southern face, raising their pups on a living cliff facing the big river.

The wolf tree's canopy became a landscape of living branches and dead wood, a maze of tiny habitats and secret places. As they foraged for beetle larvae in its decaying wood, pileated woodpeckers excavated oval cavities in the wolf tree's spreading trunks. Soon those cavities came alive: screech owls basking at their thresholds, flying squirrels peering from their shadows, gray foxes raising kits in their deepest hollows. Over the years, the cavities expanded deep into the heart of the wolf tree, becoming dens for raccoons and fishers, nests for wood ducks, explored by acorn-fatted black bears as they readied themselves for hibernation.

The wolf tree, once alone, was now an ark. Creatures beyond counting wove their lives over and around and through it.

As the wolf tree declined, the young forest changed in both subtle and profound ways. For decades, the trees in the young forest had vied against one another in the brutal race of competition. Each survivor had overcome unthinkable odds, outcompeting hundreds or thousands of their peers. But as they grew, there was room for fewer and fewer of them. Again and again, trees separated themselves from the pack, spreading branches over their neighbors, garnishing the light. Again and again, the shaded trees sank like ships, light passing through their thinning crowns and dappling the earth. Without the resources to defend themselves, the shaded trees' bodies succumbed to pests and pathogens, to the insects and the fungi and the bacteria of the necrosphere. Eventually, they fell, becoming habitat for beetles and ants, mosses and salamanders. Beech and sugar maple—the shade-tolerant trees—began to press upward from the shadows of the understory.

Windstorms and ice storms visited the mountain, toppling trees and opening gaps in the young forest's canopy. Sheaves of light bathed the forest floor, drawing currents of green life into them. Soon, new seedlings and saplings reached upward, rooted in the bodies of their fallen kin, pulling nutrients from the dead into their spreading branches. The young forest began to build its own legacies, to become complex and multigenerational, to tell a story of change. From the ashes of the ancient forest, from the oppression of the pasture ocean, the history of the forest on the mountain was being written again.

The changes in the young forest were embodied by the tree species that responded to them: yellow birch and hemlock growing from rotting wood, white pines sprouting on the mineral soil exposed by uprooted trees; oaks growing from stumps; beech rising slowly and persistently through the deep shade. Each species was nuanced and particular, each home to worlds of living things, each with the potential to carry the forest of the future in different directions. As the young forest rediscovered diversity, the trees in the forest were the outlines of an exquisite painting. Between them, a reimagined forest was being born: a living community rippling with patterns, flowing off the page, defying boundaries and dimensions.

The wolf tree was now the center of a great drama. A million lives unfurled all around it, each writing its own story, each leaving a legacy on the world of the future. Life spun outward from the wolf tree, like winged samaras from its tattered crown.

To the west, the broad valley opened toward the slender lake. Along its shoulders, a world of young forests grew atop the legacy of the pasture ocean. Though they became older and more complex each day, these forests were still children. They were still just beginning their long journey through time, still just beginning to discover what it truly means to be a forest.

Even as the forests of the broad valley regrew, they also contracted—suffering the many slow and secret deaths of global change. Driveways snaked to the ridges, houses climbing the walls of the valley. Villages became flat, gray prairies grazed by herds of shining cars. Invasive pathogens attacked the beech, the elm, and the butternut, preventing them from fulfilling their historic ecological roles, and the chestnut was missing from the forest entirely. Invasive plants crept through the forest's understory, outcompeting the native plants and displacing the species that relied on them. White-tailed deer grew more numerous each year, their browse undermining the forests' diversity. Earthworms invaded the soil, dissolving the rich humus. Even as the forests of the broad valley reached toward wholeness, they were slowly breaking, slowly losing their identity. Even as they recovered, their vitality was undermined, piece by piece.

Above the wolf tree, a logger idled his rumbling skidder, peering through the hanging boughs of a grove of hemlock. The hemlock stand was a tithe of darkness on the south-facing slope, patterned with the round beds of deer and the shuffling paths of porcupines. Black-throated green warblers and hermit thrushes sang from the canopy, and red squirrels darted across the needled ground.

Over years of summers, the skidders roared across the mountain, turning the hemlock stand and the oaks above into stumps. After a decade, they left the forest on the mountain in tatters, anemic and degraded, its rediscovered richness distant again. The loggers had reversed the race of competition, had cut all of the largest and healthiest trees, and left all the least healthy behind. Rains fell, and murky water channeled through the deep ruts in their skid trails, the remnants of the ancient soil washing away.

The loggers were not evil for cutting trees, not wrong for taking something from the forest on the mountain. They were wrong for the *way* they took it: for failing to honor the value and the beauty of the forest, for failing to take responsibility for the legacies that they left in their wake. They could have used their power to help the young forest, but instead they chose to hobble it, to tear new wounds in its already fragile body.

The loggers were not alone: everywhere, people used their power to exploit the earth's damaged ecosystems rather than to save them, to seek their own freedom at the expense of their children's. As the ecosystems of the world were degraded and destroyed, people who loved forests vilified their own power and their technology, the chainsaws and the skidders, their human nature, as things that were inherently harmful. In fact, all of these things were capable of goodness beyond measure. Though the people were the biosphere's greatest threat, they were also its greatest and only hope.

The wolf tree vibrated with manufactured sounds—engines and planes, the unending drone of the highway. Over the wolf tree's lifetime, humans had permeated and dominated every ecosystem on earth. The human world and the wild world had become a *socioecological system*, inseparably fused. Even so, as the people lived their lives, they failed to understand that their every action touched and changed the ecosystems of the biosphere and the other people of the world. They failed to understand that their choice was not *if* they wanted to have a relationship with ecosystems. Their only choice was *what they wanted that relationship to be.*

Across the wolf tree's centuries of life, the world had changed in unimaginable ways. Now it changed faster than ever, hurtling toward some inevitable and unknown future. Winters warmed and shortened, rain coming both more and less and differently than ever before, brutal storms colliding with the forest on the mountain. Forests across the earth were cleared, degraded, and polluted, their integrity undermined, shuddering with extinctions. The biosphere was shrinking, losing so many of the irreplaceable things that made this planet an oasis in a universe of darkness.

The wolf tree stood in defiance on the mountain, still daring to become *something*. It thickened its massive trunk, lengthened its branches, passed sweetness to the secret world of its roots. As carbon dioxide changed the shape and the substance of the living world, the wolf tree breathed it in, spinning it into living wood, into rich, dark soil, into habitat, into a legacy of hope.

In the little village at the foot of the mountain, a man with one good eye bought an unloved and unwanted parcel of land. With the stroke of a pen, the man owned the wolf tree and all the trees of the young forest—their roots and their branches, the wood gathered in their trunks, and the soil gathered at their feet. He owned the stumps where the red oaks once stood, the rutted skid roads, the barberry and the beech, the worms and the deer. He owned the legacies of the people who had destroyed this land's ecosystems and the lives of its first people. He owned all the harmful and unjust legacies that the forest carried into the future, like a ship on a rocking sea.

The man's blood was European, the blood of the new people of the valley, the blood of a family that once claimed ownership of hundreds of human lives. He stood on the legacies of genocide and slavery, on a mountain of privilege he did not earn, on racist and unjust legacies that he abhorred but from which he benefitted with every breath. He knew that had no more right to this land than any of his kin. But there he was.

The man met the wolf tree on a hazy summer day, his shirt dark with sweat. As he walked through the young forest, the wolf tree loomed over him like a living shadow, casting light and life everywhere around it. The man approached the wolf tree slowly as if it were a huge, tender animal. Gently, he placed a hand on its fissured bark, his gaze wandering up into its broken crown. The man imagined the doors that the wolf tree had passed through, the ancient and unimaginable worlds of which this creature was a legacy. The man himself was still a seedling, a child born into the light of an incomprehensible world. As he grew, he was learning that he could not erase the legacies of the past, could not choose the world that he inherited. He could only move forward, could only be who and where he was, could only dream of a better world and do everything in his power to make it a reality.

The man visited the wolf tree often. Sometimes he would visit when the bloodroot was in flower when the wolf tree's buds were swollen with expectation. Sometimes he would stalk by with a rifle in his hand, tracing the meandering track of a deer in the thin autumn snow. Sometimes he would pass by the wolf tree in snowshoes, his red ears poking out from beneath his hat. Always he would stop and touch the wolf tree's trunk, look upward into its twisted canopy, and sigh.

The man was learning that he was connected to everything and to everyone on earth through the responsibility he took for the present and the legacies that he left for the future. Rather than letting the legacies of the past crush him, the man draped himself with them, the weight of the burning world settling on his shoulders. Day by day, he began to build something beautiful of his brief life. Day by day, he did what he could to become like the wolf tree: something emergent, a beacon in a world of shadows.

On the edge of the clearing, a chipmunk cached an acorn in the rotting wood of a white pine stump. The next spring the acorn sprouted, becoming a tiny seedling. A pair of delicate leaves announced the seedling's identity to the world: red oak, *anaske-mezi*, the acorn tree.

Somehow, the little oak was overlooked by the deer as they waded through the meadow of hay-scented ferns on the edge of the log landing, overlooked by the loggers with their chainsaws. Somehow, the little oak raised itself upward, growing a thin trunk and tiers of branches, each tipped in lobed leaves and clusters of ornate, scaled buds.

One summer day, the man waded through the brush at the margins of the clearing, his chainsaw bucking in his hands. As he approached the little oak, he flipped down his visor, revving the saw until it screamed. Suddenly, it stopped, choking to silence with a flick of his thumb. The man looked at the little oak, not much taller than he, nodded briskly, and pulled the saw to life again. Again it screamed and again it stopped, silence ringing through the clearing. The man set the saw on the ground and stood with his arms crossed, looking at the little oak again. After a long moment, he picked up the chainsaw and walked away.

The little oak grew two strong trunks and branches that reached into empty space all around, becoming a wolf tree in its own right. The man returned often, not with the chainsaw but with a pruning saw and loppers, trimming dead branches and cutting brush at the little oak's feet. He named it the Memory Tree, and each time his truck pulled into the clearing he would measure it with his eyes like a doting father, his face full of hope.

The man and the Memory Tree grew up together. Through long summer days, the man labored in the clearing and the woods above, working hard to leave a legacy that he could be proud of. In the heat of the day, the man would rest in his chair at the base of the Memory Tree, drinking cool water and dreaming of many things that might someday be. He dreamed of healing, of emergence and abundance, of unwinding the threads of legacy that gripped the forest on the mountain. He dreamed of people who would accept responsibility for the forests of their lives and would do what was necessary, however bittersweet, to help them shine again. He dreamed of a better world.

Against all odds, the Memory Tree grew into a world of promise and opportunity: a gift to the man's children, a gift to future generations. Slowly, the man's legacy took root, like an acorn planted in the earth.

Across the world, the Khasi people of northern India built bridges from the bodies of fig trees, training vines into living structures of purpose and beauty. They began building each bridge knowing that it would take generations to complete, knowing that they would never walk across it. They did it anyway: it was their legacy, a gift to their children, a gift to future generations, a gift to an unknown future.

Behind us, the world is crumbling. Ahead of us is a roaring stream. What bridges will we build so that our children may cross the water?

4 | POWER: BECOMING A KEYSTONE SPECIES

The air is heavy and cool, the blue-eyed promise of a warm day to come. For months, life has been waiting on the mountain, impossible and inevitable. As snow drifted through the forest, as rivers glazed with ice, as bears slept in their caves under the cliffs, emergence has been promised in every bud of every tree. Now it is here, a promise fulfilled. Summer has come to the mountain again.

A rose-breasted grosbeak sings from the canopy as I climb the skid trail, my chainsaw balanced on my shoulder. All around me, trees are turning light into life, and the creatures of the forest feast. The trees' energy is carried through the air by mother birds, feeding chicks with caterpillars fattened on new leaves. It is carried outward and downward by ants, their bodies lapped up by a hungry black bear with her paws in the earth. It is carried against the current by the tiny minnows that dart up Bear Island Brook, hiding in its shaded pools. Sunlight powers this summer city, and its conduit is life.

For five years, I have walked this trail in the heat of summer and in pouring rain, in snowshoes and skis. I have walked it with my backpack sprayer on my back and my acorn-planting stick in my hand. I have walked it with my rifle, cold and heavy in my arms, the beam of my headlamp swinging over the rocks.

As I ascend the final slope, my legs burning, I smile to myself. I wonder, as I often do, how many times in my short life I will walk up this damn hill.

I pause at the first overlook, where the red pines are scarred by black bears and the huckleberry bushes are thick and brittle. Through a window in the trees, I watch the mist lift over the foothills on the far side of the broad valley, their contours tinted blue in the morning light. I adjust the chainsaw on my shoulder. The forest murmurs and squeaks and caws around me.

I begin walking again. As many times as I have walked up this hill, as much of myself as I have given to this place, I am still a visitor. As I approach, frogs and birds cease their singing and deer crash through the brush. To the animals of the forest my scent must be strange and foreign, my body perfumed with the manufactured smells of the human world. I move through the woods with the arrogance of an apex predator but none of the cunning or guile; with the power and the privilege of a creature that has never been hunted, a creature whose species rules the earth.

I crest the hill and a cool breeze touches my face, smelling of stumps and dripping lichen. It is the Anthropocene: the last doors of the world have been opened. As I carry my chainsaw through the summer woods, human influence touches every living thing, every forest on earth. My species wages war against a biosphere with the audacity to offer us life.

I set down my backpack, my jugs of gasoline and oil, resting my saw on a stump fringed with turkey tail mushrooms. As a scarlet tanager *chick-burrs* over my head, I pull out my file and begin sharpening the chainsaw's curved teeth.

Like so many things, sharpening a chainsaw is simple in theory and impossible in practice. No one can teach you to do it well; you must learn it through experience, with your hands and your body's memory, through frustration and failure and persistence. I take five scraping strokes with the file, keeping the angles just right: thirty degrees across, ten degrees down, the top of the file just licking the edge of each tooth.

This chainsaw and I have grown up together. I remember lifting it out of the display case a decade ago—its weight unfamiliar to me, its cover gleaming orange and milky-white. In the years since, I have sharpened it on stumps and on the tailgates of pickup trucks, on flat rocks and in the dry duff of countless forests, as draft horses stretched in their traces and as thunderstorms gathered overhead. I have sharpened it as I wandered in and out of relationships, in times of trauma and personal tragedy, in times of fear and anxiety and sadness and joy.

I pull the chain forward to file the next tooth. The saw rests on the stump like a dozing tiger, an earthshaking power sleeping in its gears. Thirty years ago, a chainsaw just like this laid waste to this forest, degrading it in ways that will echo through this biological community for centuries. Around me, the forest is a predator's boneyard—rotting treetops scattered like skeletons, auburn stumps rolling like skulls beneath the canopy.

I have also been harmed by a chainsaw. Last year, this saw bucked on the muddy ground as I lay bleeding on the earth, the delicate architecture of my skull crushed around my one working eye. My chainsaw hibernated in the heat of my truck as I awoke in a hospital bed in darkness, as I healed on my porch through long summer days, dreaming of the woods. Despite everything, I feel a fondness and a gentleness toward this machine. I groom it, sharpening its killer's teeth.

Metal shavings gather on the stump. Beneath the soft skin of my face, bone creeps over titanium plates like a jungle reclaiming an ancient temple. Beneath the green veneer of summer, the forest around me has regenerated from its trauma, filling its wounds with life. The forest and I mirror one another: we are each complex and injured and strange, each crooked and built of spare parts. Though we wear our scars quietly, legacies echo through us, shaping us. In spite of everything, we are reimagining ourselves and each other, learning what kind of brave and imperfect things we are as we limp indelicately into the future.

I file the last tooth and tighten the chain, unscrew the powerhead cover and shake dust from the air filter. I am a true child of this Anthropocene: part man, part machine, scarred and half-blind, young and naive and resilient and powerful. Like this forest, I will never be new again, but perhaps I may still become something of beauty.

The chainsaw leaps to life, the sounds of the waking forest lost in the engine's roar. Power runs through my hands. I inhabit the familiar, runaway feeling of holding something dangerous and untamable.

The forest is cast in gray and black, a crowd of pockmarked, diseased beech. Among them I catch glimpses of insurgent oaks, holding leaves like bundles of green fire. Decades ago, when the loggers high-graded the mountain, these oaks were saplings, too small to be noticed or cut. In the aftermath, they raced upward, surging toward the light of the canopy. They were not fast enough. The gray fingers of the beech trees reach over them now, trapping the future of this forest beneath a smothering reality.

Over the last three decades, as the rich soils of the valley grew houses and roads, as the climate changed, as a pandemic swept across the globe, as people fretted over war and famine and as technology changed the substance of their lives, the beech trees have slowly thickened their trunks, adding one slender ring of growth each year. Like the people of the valley, the beeches are not malicious; they do not mean to undermine the vitality of this forest. Like each of us, they simply seek an opportunity to live—the right of every living thing. I approach a diseased beech, its branches reaching over a promising young oak, and begin to cut.

A forest is a stone arch, both resilient and fragile, composed of many interconnected and interdependent pieces. Within this delicate structure, each species has a different role to play, but some play a bigger part than others. Some species are like the stone at the top of the arch, creatures that allow many others to exist. These are *keystone species*: the species on which many others lean, the species whose absence can cause entire communities to crumble.

In North America, the classic example of a keystone species is the beaver. Like humans, beavers are *ecosystem engineers*: a species that uses its power and its peculiar genius to change the world. Beavers build dams, creating ponds and wetlands that are vital habitat for many species of reptiles, amphibians, fish, birds, mammals, invertebrates, and plants. Besides providing unique habitat, the wetlands created by beavers improve downstream flood resilience and water quality, store huge amounts of carbon and water, build soils, and do much, much more.

Beavers were the first wildlife species in northeastern North America to feel the influence of European colonization. By the 1600s, Europeans were trapping beavers and trading for beaver pelts on a massive scale, shipping them to Europe to be used in millinery (hat-making). By 1640 beavers were largely absent from New York's Hudson Valley, and by 1670 an estimated 250,000 beaver pelts had been shipped to Europe from the Connecticut River Valley of Vermont and New Hampshire alone. Fur traders bought beaver pelts from Indigenous peoples with steel, pots, and guns, creating an economy that incited the "Beaver Wars" of the 1600s: regional conflicts between tribes over beaver-trapping grounds as beavers became scarce throughout the region. By the 1800s there were few or no beavers left in Vermont, and over the next century they became uncommon throughout their historic range.

Far below me, the big river twists through the flats of the broad valley, a patchwork of roads and cornfields, houses and villages. Four hundred years ago, the broad valley was an aquatic world, home to as many as three hundred beaver dams per square mile. I struggle to imagine the broad valley as it once was: a dynamic ecosystem, brimming with life, an amphibious world of ponds and meadows and shrubland, otters sliding down muddy banks, moose wading in the shallows. All this was created by that chubby creature with long teeth, a flat tail, and a legendary work ethic.

I bore into the beech tree, woodchips flying from the back of the saw. In a few seconds I have penetrated the heart of this living creature, the chainsaw slicing through wood layered decades before my birth. As I cut, I am traveling backward through time, flipping through the pages of the beech's book. In another moment the saw has flown back to the present, the whirring teeth piercing the far side of the trunk.

I pull my axe from my belt and pound an orange wedge into the cut, tipping the tree forward. The beech shudders and slowly falls, its fine branches raking its sisters on its way to the ground. I repeat the process again and again: cutting, boring, pounding, felling. As another beech falls, I see the light of a clearing, a patch cut glowing through the trees.

Five years ago, in the summer of the full eclipse, I walked this twisting skid trail, hanging orange flagging around the most degraded and unhealthy and hopeless patches of forest on the mountain. Five years ago, I brought loggers here and watched as they turned this patch of green forest into a pool of gaping emptiness.

I remember it like it was yesterday. In the heat of those long August days, the loggers were like beavers building a dam, flooding the forest with death. I watched as the feller-buncher severed trees with its whirling teeth, as the grapple-skidders dragged them away, drawing ripples in the dust of the trail. As the patch cuts expanded, the waters rose, drowning the soft, green plants of the forest floor—the golden thread and starflower, the *Lycopods*, the partridgeberry and the huckleberry. The waters crept upward, drowning the ants and the bumble bees, the shrubs and the small trees, the birds' nests hidden in the thickets. As the feller-buncher's saw whirred, the waters climbed the trunks of the trees, covering bustling colonies of mosses and lichens and finally suffocating the living pillars of the forest.

Five years ago, at the end of a long summer day, I walked through a finished patch cut, its waters as still and as lifeless as a new beaver pond. As the sun ebbed over Robbins Mountain, the loggers lingered on the landing, drinking cold beer on the tailgates of their pickup trucks, celebrating another day of work well done. I imagine that beavers watch the sunset over a freshly flooded valley with the same kind of satisfaction.

Five years after the loggers left in their pickups, the patch cuts shine like new mothers. They swell with raspberry and blackberry canes, with plants and trees of all different species, with birds and insects and mammals beyond counting. In the aftermath of the flood, a diverse and beautiful community has been born, singing in the light. As I watch the patch cuts glow through the trees, I can see that death has made this forest rich. I feel that I have created a beaver pond on the mountain and that everything comes to its waters to drink.

As I fill my saw with gas and oil, the patch cut is a cacophony of sound: I hear the songs of mourning warblers and veeries, redstarts and indigo buntings, the repeating triplets of a common yellowthroat, the throaty trill of a northern flicker. It brings me joy to be near the patch cut, to watch it move through time, to witness abundance where once was only dysfunction. It reminds me that in a forest, the cutting of a tree can be a rich and fertile beginning—as beautiful and as profound a kindness as the planting of an acorn.

The ghost of another keystone species haunts these hills, a species lost from the mountain forever. Passenger pigeons once visited this region in megaflocks of millions or billions of birds. Historical accounts describe these flocks as living storms, biological clearcuts fluttering across the landscape. In *The Birds of America* (1827), John James Audubon described the aftermath of a passenger pigeon flock:

> One of these curious roosting-places, on the banks of the Green River in Kentucky, I repeatedly visited. It was, as is always the case, in a portion of the forest where the trees were of great magnitude, and where there was little under-wood. I rode through it upwards of forty miles, and, crossing it in different parts, found its average breadth to be rather more than three miles. My first view of it was about a fortnight subsequent to the period when [a passenger pigeon flock] had made choice of it. . . . The dung lay several inches deep, covering the whole extent of the roosting-place. Many trees two feet in diameter, I observed, were broken off at no great distance from the ground; and the branches of many of the largest and tallest had given way, as if the forest had been swept by a tornado.

I imagine the aftermath of a megaflock of passenger pigeons: the endless acres of toppled and broken trees where once was a vibrant forest. I imagine that it would have felt as barren and as lonely as a new beaver pond, as jarring and as hopeless as a fresh patch cut. As passenger pigeons foraged and nested over millennia, I imagine how many times this would have been repeated across this landscape, how they would have covered these mountains with scars.

Like the beavers, passenger pigeons were not a keystone species just because of the death that they caused: they were a keystone species because of the life that followed. Like the patch cuts, the areas impacted by passenger pigeons would have regenerated into *early successional* forests: the brief, diverse moment in forest development that follows a large-scale disturbance. Early successional forests are a wild celebration, a feast of light for a diversity of trees, flowering plants and shrubs, providing habitat for everything from bears to moose, bats to black-and-white warblers, bees to butterflies.

Like beavers, passenger pigeons contributed to a landscape that was a shifting mosaic of forests of different ages and at different stages of development, a connected patchwork of habitats. Today, just as New England's forests—grown out of so many pastures—have not had time to develop the diversity and the complexity of old-growth forests, our landscape has not had time to rediscover the diversity and complexity of old-growth landscapes. For forests, for landscapes, to become diverse and complex again, it is not enough for trees to grow. Forests need to experience disturbances and to regenerate from them. Trees need to die.

I start the saw and walk toward another beech. If passenger pigeons still darkened the skies, we would have called them pests. In the moments after they destroyed a forest, we would have mourned the death of so many beautiful trees and condemned the creatures that killed them. Only in time would the beauty of what the passenger pigeons had done—the vibrant community manifested by their actions—have been revealed. Only then would we have seen these creatures as they truly were: a keystone species, essential and profoundly beautiful.

Today, the passenger pigeon is gone, extinct for over a century. Early successional forests are underrepresented across this region and many of the species that depend on them are in decline. Like beavers, passenger pigeons once gave life, wrapped in death, to the forest. Now they are gone.

I fell a red maple, its scarlet twigs spinning like embers. In the distance, the patch cut glows through the trees. Here on the mountain, everything vital is imperfect, everything good is bittersweet, everything precious is infused with tragedy. Every tree owes its life to the death of another. Every animal subsists off the deaths of other living things.

I move to the next tree, the chainsaw bucking in my hands. I know that the patch cut is not the same as the early successional forests that the passenger pigeons once created, but I know that it is something—that it provides some measure of refuge for the community of species that miss the passenger pigeons and the habitat that they once created. As imperfect as I am, I believe that I may still give something of value to this forest, where death cradles life in its blackened hands.

I pull the trigger. The chainsaw bites into another beech tree, woodchips spraying into the summer air. Like the passenger pigeon, I carry change on my wings.

The sun leans toward the Adirondacks, the light slicing across the mountain from west to east. I wade through a sea of felled trees, their branches arching, the saw rumbling in my hands. Down in the valley, people are drinking cold cans of beer, floating down the slow riffles of the big river. As sweat rolls down my back, a part of me wants to put down my saw and float among them. A piece of me wants to give up this struggle, to seek a life of ease and comfort, but I will not—responsibility carries me forward.

I approach a bigtooth aspen, its leaves shimmering over a gaggle of oak saplings. Aspen will always make me think of ice cream: its creamy, smooth bark, the ease with which the saw slides through its soft, white, pulpy wood. Aspen is a sugar rush, fast-growing and short-lived, as ephemeral as ice cream on a summer day.

Instead of felling the aspen I girdle it, cutting a shallow groove that just touches its bright wood. As I encircle the aspen, I sever its *cambium*, the conduit that passes the riches of its leaves down to its sinking roots. Over the next few years, the aspen will suffocate, becoming a *snag*—a dead-standing tree. Slowly, it will become a habitat for another keystone species: the pileated woodpecker, flying through the forest in its red cap, its wingbeats like shuddering gasps.

In ten years, the aspen will be a city of ants, wood-boring beetles, and tunneling insect larvae. Pileated woodpeckers will visit the aspen tree often. With its powerful beak pecking as fast as seventeen times per second, the pileated woodpeckers will mine and probe, foraging for wriggling grubs hidden in the aspen's softening flesh, following veins of richness into the heart of the tree.

As it forages, the pileated woodpecker will excavate long, oval cavities in the aspen's trunk, empty spaces that—like the patch cuts, like beaver ponds in the valley—are fated to manifest life. Tree cavities provide nesting, denning, and foraging sites for more than fifty species of birds and mammals in this forest—from barred owls and bats to wood ducks and chimney swifts, to fishers and flying squirrels and gray foxes. Like the beaver, like the passenger pigeon, the pileated woodpecker will take something entire and intact and fill it with holes. Like beaver ponds, like the aftermath of a passenger pigeon flock, like the patch cuts, these holes will prove to be generative, filling with many precious things.

As pileated woodpeckers forage, they do two seemingly contradictory things. They protect the other trees in the forest by regulating populations of pests, policing the delicate balance between trees and the insects that parasitize them. At the same time, the pileated woodpeckers are doulas of death: capitalizing on the weakness of stressed and damaged trees and ultimately facilitating their death and decline. Even as they kill trees, pileated woodpeckers provide a crucial benefit to the forest: igniting the critical process of *nutrient cycling*, the long road that turns wood into soil, that returns trees to the earth so that the forest of the future may live.

In the coming years, shards of pulpy wood will gather in piles at the aspen's feet. The aspen will drop its fine branches and then its larger branches, becoming a naked, limbless tower. The creatures of the necrosphere will spread through the aspen's shrinking body and it will be decentralized, becoming a bustling world of tiny things. In a world in which a dead tree may contain four times the biomass that it held in life, I will watch the aspen's humming cavities, wondering what it means for a tree to be alive.

Eventually, the aspen will fall. As it sinks into the earth, it will become a *nurse log*—a rich, moist seedbed for young trees and plants—and hemlock and yellow birch seedlings will sink their roots into its fertile flesh. Over the following decades, the aspen will be disassembled, its substance carried away by countless flying and crawling and growing things. Slowly, its essence will be dissolved into the soil, where it will feed trees, plants, and fungi, help the forest's soil slow, disperse, and retain water, and add to the forest's carbon pool, 60 percent of which is stored beneath my feet.

Over the coming years, the aspen will be a forest in microcosm: tracing a path from young to old to young again, a sinuous journey with no endpoint, no climax, no final destination to reach, no single purpose to embody. As it dies, the aspen will be like a beaver pond, turning from open water to meadow to shrubland to forest and back to water again, with many detours along the way. In each moment, the aspen will become something beautiful and precious and full of life—and then it will change again.

I stand back and look at the aspen, its clear trunk now marred by two shallow, parallel cuts. I have sent this tree on a beautiful journey, a path it will walk as slowly and as certainly as the sun quests toward the western horizon. Beside it, the little oaks stand in its shade, waiting to be released. As the aspen decays, white threads of fungi will reach through it, passing its essence into the roots of the oaks. Decades from now, the aspen will be gone but its legacies will remain—hidden in the oaks' trunks and their branches, in their leaves and in their red wood. in the countless acorns that they cast over the earth.

Like myself, the pileated woodpecker creates habitat for some and destroys habitat for others, protects some trees from mortality, and guides others toward the end of their lives. Like the beavers and the passenger pigeons, the pileated woodpecker's gifts are cryptic and macabre, hidden behind the dark, heavy curtains of death. The pileated woodpecker is another organ in a forest community that celebrates both life and death, another piece of an ecosystem built on both persistence and capitulation, both resilience and change.

I turn off the saw. In the distance, a pileated woodpecker hammers through the white wood of an aspen, eating ice cream in the heat of this summer day.

I set down my saw and lower myself onto the white wood of a stump, my heart drumming in my chest. My t-shirt is soaked, my arms coated with shavings. All day the chainsaw has shaken my body, has droned in my ears. Now it is quiet, and the forest seems to rest in an unearthly peace.

The sun casts lacy shadows on the trunks of the oaks, a rind of blue sky opened around each of their crowns. Around them, what was a placid forest this morning has become a tangled mess, raw and upturned and sideways. Trees twist and jumble in every direction, their leaves still green and flushed with water, still turned hopefully upward. I can no longer remember how many days I have spent like this, how many hours, how many times I have injured myself and how many times I have suffered near-misses. I have sacrificed so much, have taxed my life in so many ways, all so I could see these oaks standing like refugees from some lost, ancient culture, wrapped in silk.

On the flinty soils of Bear Island, I fight against the tides, fighting to bring light to this darkened place. In this twisted world of beech bark disease and deer browse, of deforestation and high-grading, of climate change and pollution and extinction, I am learning to accept that this world demands more from me: that I have no choice but to be a beaver, a passenger pigeon, a pileated woodpecker—to become a keystone species, singing the music of change. I search for a relationship with this forest that is both pragmatic and kind, tempered with both humility and responsibility.

In the years to come, the oaks will grow upward and out-ward, will expand their roots and their trunks and their crowns. The new gaps in the forest's canopy will regenerate, seedlings as slender as blades of grass reaching shyly toward the sun. The bodies of the fallen trees will become habitat for countless animals, plants, and insects, for gardens of mosses and lichens, for the creatures of the necrosphere and the rhizosphere. In time, I hope that my work on this summer day will be revealed to be an act of generation.

I shoulder my chainsaw and start down the skid trail toward home. My arms are heavy, my energy is spent. I have spent years of summers on this mountain, weeding around each healthy tree. Along the sides of the trail, wood tangles at the feet of every oak, their trunks slowly thickening. Everywhere, the forest has been cracked like an egg: golden and broken and suddenly boundless. I am learning that there are times when you must break something beautiful to make it shine again.

In the summer forest, deer tiptoe across the mountain, nibbling tender leaves. A fisher lopes along the ledges, nosing the checks in the rocks for porcupines. Rodents carry the spores of mycorrhizal fungi, hidden inside their tiny bodies, into the centers of the patch cuts. Salamanders hunt arthropods through caverns of rotting wood as hawks dive through schools of songbirds, their talons open. Each species is powerful, each affecting each other, each etching legacies on the forest of the future. My species is blessed and burdened with a power unlike the others: the power to shake mountains, the power of having a choice.

I believe that our true nature is to be caretakers, stewards of this earth. I believe that the true nature of our power is not to degrade and destroy but to protect this living world and to protect each other. We already have the power to bring justice and mercy and tenderness and opportunity to all things. We already have the power to transform the Anthropocene into an epoch of awakening, an epoch of regeneration, an epoch of abundance—we just need to choose to do so.

As I descend the hill, I wonder what Bear Island will be when I am an old man and my legs are no longer strong enough to carry me up the hill. In the dusk of my life, I wonder how many pieces of me will be embedded in this place forever, like stones in the soil. I hope that I will have used my power to help this forest rediscover itself, that in some small way I will have helped to build a better world.

In these moments, my life feels sacred and precious, a gift given to me so that I may help heal this crooked world. In these moments I feel like a keystone species, life spreading from me in every direction. I walk through the singing forest, dreaming of a living peace: a future written in green ink.

5 | CHANGE: THE WINDSTORM

The wind rattles the windows of my little house. Beyond the glass, the trees rock back and forth with a tightening tension, their painted leaves swinging like sheets. The rain begins in bursts, shearing sideways across the wind. It pelts the big river, threading westward through a boiling fog.

Over the mountains, the storm wracks the pine stand. The white pines have lived a life of opportunity, a green city rising from the grasses of a forgotten pasture. Now they sway in a frantic and unsteady rhythm, a mass of boughs and needles lurching in unison.

The wind rises, pressing the treetops like levers. The pines are ships at sea, sails billowing, hulls crashing through the pounding waves. With a loud crack, a pine's twin trunks twist like dancers, their hands releasing, pirouetting apart. One spins into the arms of another and then they are both falling, their roots rising from the earth like a kraken, studded with stones and bearded with dripping soil.

The wind flows into the gap in the pine stand's canopy like water into a breach. The pines have grown up together, their roots intertwined. By standing together they have weathered countless storms, their vulnerability masked by a collective resilience. Now the spell is broken. Everywhere pines fall, gaps opening and

expanding and bleeding into one another, spots becoming pud-
dles of spilled ink. The pine stand rolls untethered over the black
swells, the wind shredding it like cloth.

The sugar maple wolf tree is the captain of this sinking ship,
its feet planted as the water rises, as timbers topple, as the pine
stand keels and capsizes. For two hundred years the wolf tree's
arms have spread over this land, palms upturned regally. Now
they seem to spread in equanimity, a gesture of acceptance as the
world turns upside-down.

The winds quiet until they are whispering again. The day
dawns, needles and twigs drifting like plankton through an ocean
of muted light. The pine stand bobs in its currents, pieces of
something that can never be reassembled. The wolf tree is cleft
open and pressed into the bleeding soil. The forest has changed
forever.

Yellow and blue lights flash over tree roots, upturned against an
ashen sky. I drive through a broken world, steering around trees
and branches, power lines brushing the ground like jump ropes.
As I turn into my office, my headlights illuminate the top of a
white pine tree, splayed like roadkill on the paved shoulder.

My office is dark, the light switches dead. I sit at my desk
and drink coffee, watching the dusty glow of dawn rising over
the oaks. As I wait, I imagine the people of the county waking,
their eyes blinking, their hands fumbling in the dark. I imagine
them leaning on their counters as the sun slowly reveals that the
world outside their windows has turned sideways in the night.
I imagine their bodies tightening, their chests resonating with

a deep, unnamable frequency: the rhythm of something that should not be.

As I sip the last of my coffee, my phone starts to buzz. I speak to people with frantic voices, people who need me to understand that something deeply wrong has happened to their forest, that there must be something that I can do to fix it. I listen and make comforting sounds, eventually offering to come and take a look.

The light is still low as I start the truck and creep again through the breathless world. I pass through a suburban neighborhood, one hundred acres of identical homes planted on the memory of a sandplain forest. This morning, the streets and cul-de-sacs seem ancient and eternal, things that must always have been this way. It is an illusion. This reality, the world we inhabit, is just one ephemeral moment on a continuum of change.

One hundred thousand years ago, this land was crushed under a mile of ice, a glacier that extended hundreds of miles to the south. Thirteen thousand years ago, this land rested beneath hundreds of feet of clear, blue water: the bottom of a glacial lake that lapped the edges of a steppe roamed by wooly mammoths, wild horses, giant beavers, short-faced bears, and wooly rhinoceroses. Ten thousand years ago the megafauna were gone, their extinction coinciding with the arrival of the first people, a species previously unknown to this continent. Where the neighborhood now stands was a delta in a brackish inland sea, white sands gathering at its edges.

The sun clears the tattered treetops. People are out in their driveways, hands on their hips. Trees cross driveways and manicured lawns, torn limbs brushing the grass. Across the county, people are awakening to the aftermath of the storm, their minds straining like taut cables. They have worshipped a myth of stasis, have imagined that their reality is stable and unchanging. This morning, the world has broken its banks. Their myth lies in rags around them.

Five thousand years ago, forests were marching north, a few miles per century. As forests moved, they changed; species migrated with and within them, joining and splitting apart, navigating relationships with each other, adapting and evolving over countless generations. Although forests were moving great distances and transforming in profound ways, the change was so slow that at any moment it was imperceptible. Then, as now, generations of people walked through the forest and saw trees slowly thickening their trunks, their roots anchored firmly in the ground. Then, as now, the forest seemed as static and as unchanging as stone.

I leave the neighborhood, turning south into the broad valley. Yesterday I drove this road and leaves were floating gracefully to the ground, the oaks and the beeches colored auburn and yellow. Today the trees are bare, leaves piled in dripping dunes in the street. The storm has swept the county into winter overnight.

Three thousand years ago, the tree species of the modern forest had returned to the broad valley, but the forests were different from today's forests in every other way. Three thousand years ago, the stormwaters that coated these hills ran over the leathery leaves of massive, smooth-barked American beech trees, soaking into deep, undulating soils. They trickled through a multigenerational forest built of legacy and continuity, of thousands of years of aggradation and accumulation, death and change. The stormwaters channeled down the lichen-coated bark of ancient oaks, down dead-standing trees and fallen trunks at all stages of decomposition. The waters kissed the tongues of mountain lions and wolves, touched the soft noses of caribou and elk as they roamed a landscape without borders: a mosaic of forests of different ages and types and expressions. The stormwaters flowed into wild, meandering streams and gathered in endless beaver wetlands in the floodplains of the big river.

I merge onto the state highway, turning toward the foothills of the Green Mountains. Three centuries ago, the first people watched storms roll through the broad valley. They had lived on this land for hundreds of generations, had built complex and ancient societies here, had shaped and been shaped by this land's biological communities. Now, they reeled from a storm of unprecedented ferocity: waves of disease swept over and through them, turning vibrant villages into cemeteries, casting entire nations into times of tragedy and uncertainty and upheaval. As the first people suffered, the new people gnawed at the edges of their world, an unstoppable tide of genocide and assimilation and displacement pressing further into the body of this abundant continent each day. The first people's land, their culture, and the substance of their lives was being taken from them. Their forests were soon to follow.

Two centuries ago, the first people and the ancient forests had been nearly exiled from the broad valley. A white tide had washed over the land, an epidemic of deforestation and exploitation and extinction. Over the course of a single human generation, a boundless and bountiful and wild landscape had been replaced by an endless pasture, a world of hedgerows and fences and millions of shaggy sheep.

I take the River Road, tracking the big river through fields of corn stubble. One century ago, the sheep farms had become dairies. As long, low barns sprouted across the county, white pines had reclaimed the most marginal pastures, had matured and been reaped like corn, had been turned into fields of stumps again. Stacks of pine boards fringed the shores of the long lake, ready to be shipped down the Champlain Canal to New York and beyond. The opulence of the 1800s had exhausted the land; the topsoil was gone, bare rock exposed, white sands rising in dunes against tilting fence posts.

As I cross the big river, its currents muddied and clotted with debris, I wonder how we arrived at this moment. The day dawns across a world that is the legacy of countless storms, the legacy of countless moments like these painted over unfathomable expanses of time. We stand in an ancient river, its waters flowing endlessly around our feet.

The gravel driveway is littered with pine boughs, their delicate needles brushing the wheels of the truck. Yesterday, a pine stand shaded this road. Today it lies in pieces, pitch bleeding from fragrant white wood, the driveway cast in a stark, piercing light. The wind carries drifts of pine needles across the gravel and for a moment I feel like I am in a desert, winding through fingers of blowing sand.

As I creep the truck down the driveway, I can see the history of this place. The story is familiar: seventy years ago, this road passed through a century-old pasture dotted with brown cattle. For generations, a family of farmers milked a few dozen cows here, carting their milk to the creamery in town each day. In the 1950s the family was unable to afford the refrigerated bulk milk tank required by law and, like two-thirds of the dairy farms in

Vermont, they sold their herd. The cattle are gone, over the following decades the pasture returned to forest.

Fifty years ago, this road passed through a sea of white pine trees no taller than my waist, their red roots piercing the compacted sod. As the stand of young pines grew, as their trunks thickened, as their tasseled branches lengthened, white pines colonized abandoned pastures all across Vermont.

The first colonists on this landscape told stories of white pines of mythical proportions: two hundred feet in height and six feet in diameter, their trunks perfect, straight columns of white wood. The white pines were part of what drew the new people to this place, part of what ignited the initial waves of colonization—a resource that timber-starved Europe could not ignore.

The white pines of the abandoned pastures were different from the ancient pines. They were twisted and multistemmed, a symptom of being attacked again and again by the white pine weevil. Their bark was streaked with pitch, a symptom of the nonnative white pine blister rust. Their crowns were thin and anemic, a symptom of white pine needlecast. Whereas the ancient pines had grown on gravels and sands, along the long lake and on the shoulders of the broad valleys, these white pines grew everywhere, their abundance owed to opportunism—a unique ability to colonize abandoned fields. In a region in which nearly every forest was a field just decades ago, they thrived.

A pine trunk lies across the driveway. I park the truck and climb out, the air sharp with the smells of pine pitch and turned earth. A warm breeze touches my face. The pine stand beside the road is a study in devastation, purple-black trunks twisted and shattered and layered across one another, the dripping earth torn open by their upturned roots. The few trees that remain standing are as naked as telephone poles, stripped of their branches and needles, or have been snapped fifteen feet off the ground.

Everything is quiet. As I walk down the driveway, I feel a wave of nostalgia. I am in a city on a holiday, the streets empty, the stores closed, nowhere to go and nothing to be done. Everything holds its breath, suspended for one brief and precious moment in time.

Gradually, my nostalgia is replaced by the buzz of anticipation. Like most foresters, I am a *disturbance ecologist*: I study death, disturbance, and change, the way that the resilience of the forest expresses itself in moments like these. In forestry school, I learned about *succession*: the process of forest development, the way that forests change over time. In my textbooks, succession was a linear path, beginning with a large-scale disturbance—a windstorm or a forest fire, an insect or disease outbreak, a clearcut, a pasture—and ending with a *late successional*, or old-growth, forest. I committed the stages of succession to memory: *stand initiation* led to *stem exclusion* led to *understory reinitiation* led to *late succession*. Each stage was as predictable as a recipe in a cookbook.

As I learned about succession, I began to mythologize old-growth forests. Old-growth forests were everything that modern forests were not—ancient and mysterious, complex and diverse and resilient. I began to see every stage of succession as a stepping stone on the path toward this final destination; old growth was the end of the line, the pinnacle, the climax, the fullest expression of a forest. Though I did not yet know it, as I sacralized old-growth forests I was trading one misunderstanding for another.

A muddy brook winds through the blowdown. A few miles to the north, the big river is swollen against its banks, its currents gnawing at the edges of its channel as persistently and as subtly as a dog with a bone. The river, like a forest, is a dynamic community that refuses to be linear. Over millennia, the river and the biological community that surrounds it have adapted to change: to cut through the soil of the floodplains, to deepen, lengthen, and change course, to cast off islands and oxbow ponds like feathers in the wind. The community of the river has adapted to the floods and ice flows, to the drowning waters of spring, to the sheaves of soil layered like new skin on its banks each year. There is no climax, no perfect form for the river to achieve. It simply changes, as it always has and as it always will.

In the decade since I left forestry school, I have learned that forests are like rivers. Succession is not a linear, one-way journey; it is an endless process, a cycle that forests pass through again and again. Each stage of succession is a destination, each providing habitat for entire communities of species, each supporting vital natural processes, each a universe of unique and irreplaceable values. None is a means to an end. Like the big river, the forest has no endpoint to attain, only a meandering path of detours and dead ends, a continuum of change that it will navigate forever. Today, after seven decades of traveling down the road of succession, the pine stand has begun again. It is not a failure, not a loss—just another bend in the river, another new and promising beginning.

I watch the pine stand, wondering why it is so tempting to place lines and edges and corners on this living world. I now understand that forests do not read the textbooks or follow the rules, that succession is a framework built to understand systems defined by their irregularity, their variability, their unpredictability. I now understand that succession is like my path through life:

a pattern within which each moment is novel and strange, each defined by trials and challenges and threats and opportunities, each a jumping-off point capable of carrying me to many unexpected and vital places. As I reimagine forests, I have learned that a true understanding of them is hidden between the lines, in the pages between their pages.

On the front steps of her house, I meet Sarah, her eyes wide. I follow her down a worn footpath across her yard and into the woods. We have only walked for a minute before the trail vanishes entirely, lost in a sea of fallen pines. Sarah stops, inhaling sharply. I can tell this was a trail that she walked each morning, a tender ritual that she kept for a decade or more. Now the trail is gone, and Sarah's life has changed forever.

Ahead, the pine stand is a study in death and disorder. Yesterday, this forest was easy to love: a garden of evenly spaced trees, an open, park-like understory. There was no brush to press through, no fallen logs to weave around. Sarah moved through the pine stand easily, taking long, sweeping strides. In a chaotic world, the neatness of the forest called to her, touched her heart, soothed her.

Yesterday, Sarah saw this forest as an island in a dynamic sea—one thing, at least, that would never change. Today, the pine stand is a community in tragedy, colored with the emptiness of loss: the loss of familiarity, of order, of simple beauty. Today, Sarah's instincts are telling her that this is no longer a safe and beautiful place, that this is no longer *her* place, that this forest is a stranger. Something has been broken. Something is deeply wrong.

Being a steward of a forest is full of moments like this—moments that are tragic, dissonant, strange. As we weave through the fallen forest, I think of the people across the county who feel just as Sarah feels this morning. Everywhere, the people of the world have imagined that the forests of their lives are stationary things and that death, disorder, and change are failings. Everywhere, people have projected their anxiety with changes in their own lives onto forests—systems within which change is as vital as trees and plants and animals. Everywhere, people have projected their anxieties about their own mortality onto forests within which death is a profound and beautiful rite of life.

We reach the top of a little rise and pause. Below us is an ocean of shattered and upended trees, the pine stand resting in pieces. From above, I can see the faint lines of the old fields, the grid of stone walls that once divided these pastures, revealed again.

Yesterday, we would have stood on this rise and looked over a canopy as flat and as regular as a field of cut grass. We would have watched a sea of green needles sway in the wind, would have listened to them whispering against each other. We would have seen a forest defined by thousands of beautiful, vital pine trees: the massive, living beings that midwifed this land's impossible transformation from pasture to forest.

Now it is time for the pines to become something else. Through all this loss, I can see that death has offered this forest a precious opportunity, that clasped inside this moment is a pearl, waiting to fill the forest with its beauty. I spread my arms wide, summoning the courage to smile as I describe the feast, the celebration to come.

"This is so exciting!" I tell Sarah, clapping my hands together. "In three years, this space will be filled with young trees, raspberries and blackberries and flowering plants. There will be white-throated sparrows and chestnut-sided warblers singing and insects buzzing everywhere. This empty space will be filled with life."

Sarah looks at me and then down at the broken and silent pine stand. While I can almost see the future of this forest—the saplings glimmering through the naked trunks of the pines, the flashing songbirds, the butterflies drifting from flower to flower—she cannot. To her, this is a funeral, and I am a crazed prophet, summoning life from a corpse. I drop my hands and continue, my voice softer.

I tell Sarah that this new generation of trees is just one of the many ways that this forest will change. As the trees in the young forest trace the winding path of succession, the forest community will experience *ecological succession*—each change in the structure and the composition of this forest manifesting new habitats for countless living things. Billions of organisms of thousands of species will build lives around the young trees and the dead wood, the snags and the canopy gaps, the shrubs and the plants that will rise from this wreckage.

I gesture toward the pine trees lying across the upturned earth. "These trees are not the forest," I say, my hands open. "Your forest is still here. It has not been lost, only changed. This is a good thing."

I try to explain how, through so many endings, this young forest is just beginning to deepen itself, just beginning to rediscover what it truly is: a natural community enriched by change and defined by scars, a living system built for a world in which stasis is a myth and stability an illusion. Over millennia, this forest has weathered storms beyond counting, each time responding by becoming something new. This one will be no different.

Sarah drops her eyes, and I stop talking. We turn and descend the hill in silence. I wonder how many times the world will change before we learn that the world *is* change. I wonder how long we will struggle against change like a fish on a line, rail against it like children, build fortresses of sand around ourselves only to see the waves of change dissolve them again and again. I wonder how long it will take for us to learn that stability is vulnerability, that resilience is strength.

I can tell that for Sarah, in this moment, hope seems beyond reach. The pine stand is a seed in her hand, hard and cold and tiny—she cannot imagine that it will ever open, that life will ever bloom from this lifeless thing. Today, this forest is a seed that cannot possibly become a flower.

We turn a corner and Sarah gasps. Ahead of us, a huge sugar maple wolf tree has been torn in half. One of its twin trunks remains upright, leaning precariously, its branches stripped. The other lays across the earth, buried by layers of shattered pines. Somehow, the wolf tree still stands proudly, its bark decorated with pine needles like a robe of green flowers.

Sarah holds her hand over her mouth. Yesterday, the wolf tree was a spotlight in the shade of the pine stand, an island in a sea of darkness. I can tell that Sarah had a special relationship with this tree, that it was important to her. I can tell that each morning Sarah's feet carried her down her trail to this place, her body drawn instinctively toward this elder, this living legacy, this tender place in the heart of the forest.

I have lost trees like this, and I know that it is like losing a friend. I watch what remains of the wolf tree and remember the Red Queen, the massive elm of my childhood, finally succumbing to Dutch elm disease. I remember the Intervale Avenue hackberry, a pillar of my life in the city, uprooted by a summer thunderstorm.

The wolf tree's standing trunk bobs like a buoy, a sliver of living wood holding it upright. The wolf tree is centuries old, a survivor of the endless pasture. It persisted as the pasture went fallow and as the forest regrew, as the young pines rose precipitously around it. For two hundred years, the wolf tree has been an ecosystem engineer, a habitat, a natural community, a landscape in microcosm. It has left an indelible imprint on this forest and its biological community. Even now, it persists.

Sarah does not know that for decades the wolf tree has leaned toward death, inhabiting the cryptic expanses of the perimortem period. As Sarah visited the wolf tree, microscopic threads of fungi spread through its hollow trunk, bacteria simmering in its softening wood. As she touched its fissured bark, wood-boring beetles burrowed through the wolf tree's body, larvae sketching galleries on its supple cambium. As she sat in the wolf tree's shade, pileated woodpeckers foraged in its canopy, decorating its trunks with oval cavities. Even as Sarah's relationship with the wolf tree bloomed, its identity was being subtly transformed: carried away by opportunists and associates, parasites and predators, each taking a tithe of the wolf tree's riches.

I tell Sarah how, in death, the wolf tree will be a mother. Even as the last glimmers of the wolf tree's *biological life* fades, its *ecological life* will persist; across decades, the wolf tree will be the body of a whale on the ocean floor, a feast for the creatures of the world. Countless lives will be born from her body, each as unique and as precious as her own. As she decays, the wolf tree will be decentralized, becoming a cooperative of millions of tiny things, the foundation of a complex and precious living community. As biologist E. O. Wilson writes, "Every corpse is an ecosystem."

I watch the wolf tree and know that, as in the pine stand, nothing has ended here. The wolf tree has simply opened another doorway, crossed another threshold. Now, it walks down another long hall.

Sarah and I crawl under and over fallen trees, weaving deeper into the belly of the forest. We cross a stone wall and suddenly the forest changes, becoming a stand of hardwoods with a vaulted canopy of oak and ash, sugar maple saplings rising through the understory.

I can tell that, 120 years ago, a farmer walked this stone wall, pulling a strand of barbed wire from west to east. In the years that followed, the southern pasture—someday to become the pine stand—was grazed by cattle as this northern pasture roughened and regenerated, eventually growing its own stand of white pines. Sixty years ago, as the southern pasture began to go fallow, the pine trees in the north pasture had become large enough to cut. The farmer's sons began to fell the pines and buck them into logs, to hitch them to their tractor and drag them to the roadside, to mill them into lumber to repair the farm's many tilting barns and sheds. As more and more of the pines were cut, generations of hardwoods began to regenerate, to fill the understory and then the midstory, creeping skyward as the canopy opened. Thirty years ago, the farm family hired a logger to cut the last of the pines in the north pasture. As the last load of pine logs were trucked down the old road, the northern pasture had completed another remarkable transformation. Where once was an ancient forest, where once was a pasture, where once was a pine stand stood a diverse, multigenerational stand of hardwoods.

The storm has touched the hardwood stand differently. Gaps punctuate the canopy like missing teeth—the forest grins at us crookedly. The canopy of the hardwood stand is the roof of an ancient barn, the morning light streaming through openings of different shapes and sizes, casting ragged shadows on the forest floor. Where the pine stand has failed as explosively as a river breaching a dam, the hardwood stand has weathered the storm like a river in its floodplain, accepting small changes to buffer itself from large ones. The hardwood stand is a testament to the resilience that forests find in diversity, the wisdom of being many things at once.

I tell Sarah that, like the openness of the pine stand, the gaps in the hardwood stand's canopy will regenerate, filling with young trees. In ten years, the smaller gaps will be clusters of *shade-tolerant* trees like hemlock, beech, and sugar maple—species that are slow growing and capable of surviving in near or complete shade. In the larger gaps, *midtolerant* species like white ash, red oak, and yellow birch—species that outcompete the shade-tolerant trees in larger openings but are unable to grow in the complete shade—will thrive. Across the stone fence, the glut of light in the pine stand will manifest *intolerant* species like white birch and aspen and pin cherry—species that will only grow in the open.

After picking our way slowly through the pine stand, Sarah and I move through the hardwoods easily, skirting the scattered blowdowns. We stop where a huge red oak lays across the earth, brittle leaves still clinging to its branches. The oak's rootball towers over us, a fist of wet soil studded with silver stones, humus trailing from its edges like tufts of wiry hair. As the oak fell, it rampaged through the canopy, its wide crown tearing through a group of sugar maples. Some of the sugar maples are trapped under the oak's rusty curls, their trunks ending in rootballs of their own. Others stand like headless statues, their trunks snapped twenty feet off the ground.

Once, the fallen oak was a seedling in the understory of a pine stand, a tiny and vulnerable thing. Once, it had the strength and the fortune to live an impossible dream, rising above thousands of others to reach the canopy. Once, it lived a beautiful life, its crown echoing with birdsong, its branches bowing under the weight of thousands of perfect, round acorns.

Like the pine stand, like the wolf tree, the death of the oak does not mean that its life was in vain. Like the pine stand, like the wolf tree, the oak has not been lost or diminished—it has simply changed, becoming a promise of different things to come. In a few years, the gap that it tore in the canopy will fill with insects, pursued by darting flycatchers. Deer will meander around the fallen oak, grazing tender plants unknown to the shaded forest. In will come the predators: the spot on the end of the weasel's tail bobbing as it sprints along the oak's trunk, the green eyes of a bobcat stalking the edge of the gap, the hawk perched on the frayed spire of a broken sugar maple. Over the years, the oak will sink like a ship, its trunk tattooed with moss, yellow birches shining goldenly atop its decaying roots.

Today, the gaps in the hardwood stand's canopy are empty, a hundred tears in the living fabric of the forest. In a decade they will have been sewn together with threads of countless colors: a gradient of light conditions manifesting a diversity of tree species, a diversity of tree species manifesting a diversity of living things, a diversity of living things manifesting a vibrant and resilient community. The spaces between the trees will be revealed to be as generative and as precious and as beautiful as the trees themselves.

I can tell that I have said enough. We walk back to the house in silence, over the stone wall and past the wolf tree, through the chaos of the blowdown. I want to tell Sarah that everything will be as just it was, and that nothing like this will ever happen again, but I know that it is not true. As long as there have been forests, there have been windstorms and ice storms and forest fires, pests and parasites and pathogens. Storms will visit this forest forever.

I hope that next summer Sarah will build a new trail. I hope that it will thread through the blowdown, visit the wolf tree and travel across the stone wall, curl past the fallen oak and through the dappled light of the hardwood stand. I hope that as Sarah walks the new trail each day, she will witness the forest's resilience: impossible and inevitable. I hope that, like her forest, she will regenerate, the holes in her life filling with new things—different and strange but still, perhaps, beautiful.

I hope that one day Sarah's great-grandchildren will walk the trail and see a forest that is every stage of succession at once, a forest that is always breaking, a forest that is alive and glorious with change. I hope that they will walk among ancient trees, past snags laced with oblong cavities, their crowns lying at their feet.

I hope that Sarah's great-grandchildren will carry the legacies of this moment—that this storm will have taught Sarah that death is a beginning, that change is a gift, and that she will pass this understanding to future generations. I hope that when a storm comes to this forest, Sarah's great-grandchildren will walk through its aftermath, blessing the fallen and broken trees, the canopy gaps twinkling like stars in a galaxy of shadows. I hope that they will understand how a forest lovingly kindles the flames of change, and that they will teach their children.

I leave Sarah on her doorstep and walk back down the driveway. I think of her as I climb into my truck, as I turn onto the town road. A new day has broken, and Sarah's world has been upturned. For a time, she may lose herself in the grief of this moment. Then, she will be like a forest—wrapping the change around her, discovering what kind of brave and resilient thing she truly is.

This is what it means to be resilient: to mourn a thousand endings and celebrate a thousand beginnings, to be as strong as steel and as soft as warm butter, to practice both resistance and acceptance, to cradle both life and death in our arms. I wonder what it would mean to reimagine change: to see it as not something that visits us but as something that defines us, to see it not as an antagonist but as a friend.

I drive back through an expansive landscape, a vast planet, a diverse and interconnected human community. I drive through a world that is miraculous and suffering, beautiful and degraded, perfect and flawed. I drive through a world in which every towering redwood was once a tiny seedling, a world in which every old-growth forest was once a young forest and will be one again. I drive through a world in which the forests of our lives have been, and are becoming, countless unimaginable things.

I turn toward Bear Island, the broken forest of my heart. Around me, the forests of the broad valley are lakes of color, rippling in the wind. Peeking out from behind these moments is what life truly is: to change, to become ourselves, to have the courage to change again.

6 | FREEDOM: A BRANCH ON A TREE, A TREE IN A FOREST

We drive south in Navah's old Camry, the midsummer air crowding thickly around us. The orange sun rises over the sitting-place mountain, coloring the fog in the meadowed valleys. My world is soft and sweet and expanding; I am young and in love and I work in the woods.

The highway carries us away from our apartment in Burlington, away from the little city on the long lake. We drive toward the rising sun, following the shifting path of the big river through the broad valley. As we approach Bear Island, mist hangs over Stimson Mountain like torn cloth, and for a moment the land is an old woman wrapped in a white blanket, her hands on her knees. In moments like these, I wonder what other names this mountain has carried over the millennia, and I ache to know.

Somewhere high above, the orchard trees are just beginning to probe slender roots through the dry, compacted soils of the clearing. The Memory Tree is still a sapling, eight feet tall, its trunk still slender enough to wrap my fingers around. The patch cuts on the mountain are still fresh and empty, still waiting to fill with life.

In the year that I have owned Bear Island, I have just begun to heal this place. Each weekend I visit Bear Island, each weekend giving a piece of myself in the hope that this land will someday be vibrant and resilient again. As I watch the forest on the mountain fly by my window, I allow myself to imagine that the clearing is an orchard of apples and pears and chestnuts, their limbs laden with fruit. I imagine that some of the thousands of acorns that I planted in the patch cuts last October have become towering oaks, their crowns heavy with acorns of their own. I imagine that the Memory Tree is massive and ancient, its branches reaching in every direction. I imagine that everything I have given to this place, all the seeds that I have scattered over this patch of fallow ground, have taken root. On this summer day, my dreams seem both distant and close enough to touch.

In five seconds, the highway carries us past Berta Brook and Bear Island Brook, past the old farmhouse and barn, past the little village of Bolton Flats, across Joiner Brook. In five seconds, the highway has carried us past Bear Island, and we are away.

I watch the familiar shape of Stimson Mountain fade in the rearview mirror. In five seconds, each car on this highway passes by a forest of boundless complexity and bottomless depths, a forest that will change and grow as I become old and small and as my children have children of their own. In five seconds, they pass a forest whose fullness will always elude me, a forest that I will spend a lifetime trying to understand and to make just a little more alive.

We leave the broad valley, rolling over heights and into strange watersheds. The highway turns and tracks south, tracing the course of *gweneguitegw*, the long river, the river of my childhood. As we leave Vermont the trees and the forests gradually change. Maple is replaced by oak, the ivory bark of sycamore shining in the floodplains, dark thickets of red cedar huddled in old fields.

Through the windshield I peer into the green folds of alien mountains, the summer woods of Connecticut, Pennsylvania, New Jersey. I imagine that every five seconds I am passing a forest with the complexity, the beauty, the mystery of Bear Island. Every five seconds I am passing a world of stories baked into the rocks, dramas unfolding through the pores of the soil. Every five seconds life is scampering over logs, flickering from branch to branch. Every five seconds is another unique and irreplaceable ecosystem, turning through the peeling expanses of time.

The highway is an asphalt savanna, herds of cars and trunks stampeding over a gray expanse. Around us, the people of the world are going to work, to the grocery store, bringing their children to school. Each of them experiences joy and hardship, trauma and fulfillment, their lives filled with anxiety and purpose. They pass us by like the forests along the highway; through their windows, we catch glimpses into countless unimaginable and vital realities.

Humans are *unitary* organisms. Each of us is an individual, our biology united toward a singular purpose. Around me, each car speeds on a divergent path. Each person is at the wheel of their own life, on some mission of personal importance. Each person seeks freedom: the freedom to be happy, fulfilled, and comfortable, to find meaning and empowerment, the freedom to be and to become themselves.

Trees are *modular* organisms, comprising many repeating *modules*. Within a tree each branch is a kind of a suborganism, an entity with the autonomy to compete with neighboring branches, to support its own energetic economy, to live and to die alone. For this reason, some researchers and botanists have reimagined trees as a *colonial organisms*: more like colonies, or collectives, than individuals.

The autonomy of branches is real and is also an illusion. Each branch is connected to a trunk, to a common root system, to a community of other branches. A branch cannot live without the water and nutrients channeled through the tree's root system, without the sturdy architecture of the trunk, without the many processes and properties and functions provided by the tree as a whole. The fate of each branch is bound to the fate of the other branches, nested within the fate of a larger collective entity.

The relationship between branches and trees is a fractal, a pattern that repeats itself at different scales. Within a forest, each tree is an autonomous individual, competing with neighboring trees for light and resources, for the ability to reproduce and to pass its genes to future generations. At the same time, a tree cannot live alone. Each tree is dependent on the seed dispersers and pollinators, the invertebrates and their predators, the bats and the birds, the necrosphere and the rhizosphere, the creatures and the processes and the functions of the forest community. A tree cannot stand alone.

Across the blinking lines of the highway, I watch the people in their cars and trucks as they seek their unitary freedom, living enigmatic and separate lives. Though they are as different from me as a sugar maple is from a yellow birch, we are branches on the same tree—both free and connected, both autonomous and in relationship with one another.

Rain taps the windshield, a warm and sudden summer shower. The rainclouds above us are the gathered breath of countless forests, a by-product of the miraculous process of photosynthesis. I daydream of Bear Island, picturing raindrops wetting the leaves of an oak, meandering down its trunk and sinking into the soil at its feet. As a ray of sun pierces the clouds, I imagine the same raindrops drawn into the oak's roots and up the fibers of its trunk, into its branches, its twigs and finally its lobed leaves, where they are lost to the air as vapor. I imagine the mist from the raindrops drifting upward, drawn into high clouds. I imagine the clouds soaring over some distant crop field, the raindrops condensing and falling on some green field of wheat.

Though we have changed the substance of our atmosphere, changed when and where and how the rain comes, we cannot change the fact that nothing can live without rain, and that rainclouds cannot live without forests. As cars pass us by, I imagine that the wheat from that distant field fills the bodies of the people in the cars on the highway. I imagine that my work at Bear Island has nourished them in some small way as they race through their complex and precious lives.

We listen to audiobooks and watch the world go by, the Camry's tires licking endless acres of pavement. No matter how many hundreds of miles we drive, each highway exit drops us into the same place: the same boxy outlets, the same chain restaurants simmering in the summer heat. Though we pass through places with distinct cultures, distinct histories, distinct ecologies, there is nothing that distinguishes them from anywhere else in America.

As we travel farther south, the blights of global change become louder. I see the huge trunks of tree-of-heaven, the countless ash trees killed by the emerald ash borer, the bittersweet vines swarming over the roadsides. I see forests with understories as open and as barren as parking lots, ecosystems disintegrating from the impacts of massive deer overpopulations. I see forests fragmented by homes and driveways and development, the sprawling neighborhoods of single-family houses, the green lawns where once were woods and wetlands. Everything crescendos as we dive further into the thrumming mass of the Eastern Seaboard, where concrete cities are connected by concrete highways, the remnants of ecosystems lying like carcasses by the sides of the road.

I think of my home in Vermont, where all these problems are present but more muted. The invasives, the deer, the development creep north, slowly sapping the integrity of the forests that I love. Such is the nature of people that most will not recognize these problems until they are untenable, until it is too late. We do not need to imagine what Vermont would be like if we fail to address these threats—if we fail to control the invasives, to lower the deer populations, to restrict the development. All we need to do is drive south.

In Virginia, we finally leave the highway and find our hotel amid an ocean of pavement stretching to the horizon. We check into our room, unpack, wash our weary bodies. As the afternoon sun lingers, I set out to explore this strange place.

Heat shimmers from the blacktop. I try to imagine this land as it once was: a mosaic of forests and wetlands, home to peoples with a culture and history deepened over hundreds of generations. With their freedom and their power, European colonizers destroyed this forest, the bodies of these people and the substance of their lives. With their freedom and their power they enslaved humans from across oceans and used them to turn these forests into pastures and hayfields and cropland. The legacies of genocide and slavery are baked into the soil here, mixed with the legacies of ecosystem exploitation and destruction that echo throughout this modern world.

On this summer day, the forest is gone, transformed into parking lots and box stores. The wetlands are constructed ponds at their frontiers, furred with tasseled *Phragmites*. I lean in the shade of a Norway maple, watching the people come and go, wondering how this place came to be.

Centuries ago, this land was stolen, cleared, and transformed, passed from farm family to farm family until it was sold to a developer for a tidy profit. The developer paved it and sold it again for another nice return. The chain stores rose from the asphalt, stocking shelves with cheap products produced in countries with less stringent environmental regulations, human rights laws and labor laws, their products subsidized by the suffering of peoples and species and ecosystems somewhere far away. The box stores outcompeted the local businesses, extracting profits that enriched distant executives and shareholders and providing low-paying jobs to local people. Like the invasive plants by the highway, these stores soon dominated this landscape— smothering its uniqueness, replacing diversity, complexity, and abundance with a sterile and lifeless monoculture.

I cross the pavement desert, this profound expression of individual freedom. I wonder how a single person can be allowed to make choices that undermine the resilience, the self-reliance and the freedom of countless others. I wonder how a single person can be allowed to become wealthy by destroying a forest—an ecosystem that could have enriched and sustained the lives of thousands of people and trillions of organisms for centuries. In pursuit of their own freedom, a few people have stripped the bark from the social and biological tree from which we all branch, chipped away its wood, studded it with nails. They have flourished while the rest of the world withers.

The Virginia heat assaults me from every direction, but I shiver. I imagine this place as it may once have been, the living things that would have roamed and fluttered and buzzed through this green world on a day like today. On a summer morning, the leaves of the trees would have been beaded with dew, the tiny roots of plants and shrubs and tree seedlings threading through the dark soils at their feet. I imagine the living things that would have found refuge here, the clouds that would have been seeded by its waters. I am haunted by secret disappearances: the countless lives that never had a chance to exist.

Ranks of cars shine in the sun. Some are old and some are new, some patched and rusty and others opulent and sleek. The people come and go, resolved in their new economy, their new ecology, their new culture. Each believes that they are an independent branch, racing against the others, grasping for individual freedom. They have been told that the only measures of their success are the riches that they take for themselves: the wealth and the power, the happiness and the freedom that they can mine from this living world. It is not true. Even in this disjointed reality, they are as connected to each other and to the ecosystems of the biosphere as the branches of the same tree.

Far to the north, Bear Island grows and changes. I have spent each weekend this summer living a different vision of freedom—coated in sweat and sawdust, spending the finite energy of my body to help the forest on the mountain become strong and supple, a greater gift to the creatures and the people of the earth. I have worked myself to exhaustion in the hope that I am helping to manifest a society where we seek individual freedom within the context of collective freedom, where we reach toward emergence and empowerment in a world where everyone is empowered, where everyone is free.

The sun tilts westward. I walk back toward the hotel, weaving through parking lots darkened by the square shadows of the box stores. The people move like strings of ants: into the stores with empty hands, into the parking lot with plastic bags bulging with foreign treasures. I watch them as they prosecute their strange and distant lives, as they live and thrive and struggle in the world they have been given.

I remind myself that this is a piece of the same world that I love and that I wish to save, that these people and I are branches on the same tree, trees in the same forest. I watch as the people cross the parking lots, each carrying their own needs and desires, each owning a piece of our shared reality. Each person holds a tiny piece of an unthinkable power: the freedom to destroy ecosystems or to protect them, to destroy or to protect each other, to destroy or to protect the people and the world of the future. Our roots are intertwined. Like the branches on a tree, like the trees in a forest, it is up to us to become something together.

The driveway is flanked by pin oaks, their branches arrayed in perfect, symmetrical whorls. I pull onto the shoulder of the paved road and unfold the map.

I am back in Vermont, watching the tail of another endless summer fade away. Autumn is finally coming, and a few red maples are already aflame on the forested flanks of Bryant Hill. I am here in my capacity as a service forester, to inspect this parcel for compliance with a tax abatement program. The notes taken by my predecessor a decade ago say that this is a family woodlot, a piece of an unbroken forest that ranges over the mountains to Jonesville, just a few miles from Bear Island.

I glance down at the map again. I am looking for a logging road that should be little more than tire tracks in the sod. Instead, there is a manicured driveway, freshly graded and coated with gravel. I put the truck into gear and turn cautiously onto it, passing under the spreading branches of the oaks and across a mowed meadow. At the field's edge, the driveway turns upward into the forest.

A westerly wind tousles the leaves on the trees, battered and torn after a long summer. The driveway carries me over ridges and valleys and brooks, through stands of white pine and hemlock and sugar maple. With each turn, my grip on the steering wheel tightens. The road is endless, a probing vine cutting deeper and deeper into the heart of the forest.

Finally, the driveway ends, opening into clear blue sky. The beginnings of a house perch at the edge of a cliff, its walls naked, its new bones rising from the soil. Around it, the ridge has been clearcut, exposing a sweeping vista of the broad valley.

I park the truck and step out to take in the view. From the cliff's edge, the valley is a patchwork of colors and textures and shapes. Fields spread along the floodplains of the big river stippled with rows of corn stubble. Forests climb upward from the blank faces of meadows, their green bodies dotted with shining houses. The brick buildings of Richmond Village gather in the locus of the valley, the silver ribbons of the highway just beyond.

I watch the big river curl through the valley, her braided currents flowing west. Her floodplains are dry and marbled with roads, cars crawling along them like shining beetles. Like most of the eastern United States, about 80 percent of Vermont's forests are privately owned. There is no test to pass to become a landowner, no competencies required. Each comes to their land with their own beliefs and biases, understandings and misunderstandings, and each is granted profound freedoms.

The valley below, once an endless expanse of forests and wetlands, is composed of hundreds of privately owned parcels. From above, many of the boundaries between parcels are invisible, the forest blending seamlessly together. Others are sharp and clear. Three centuries ago, the first boundaries drawn through the broad valley were meaningless. The ancient forests were a single body, their bones and their blood spanning the lines on the survey maps with ease. In the years since, the boundaries have proved to be self-fulfilling prophecies: at the iron pin, the stone fence, the rusted strands of barbed wire, the red-painted axe blazes, the people of the valley have accepted that the freedoms of one person end and those of another begin. Over hundreds of years, shaped by the freedoms of countless landowners, the parcels have followed divergent paths. They have become different things.

A few sugar maple wolf trees have been left on the ridge, alone again, their leaves sunlit and shimmering. Over centuries, the endless forest has been fragmented by roads and driveways, fields and lawns, by the architecture and the infrastructure of humanity. Houses and their tailing driveways increasingly infiltrate the forests that remain, winking like shards of glass in a bed of moss. The valley below is both connected and divided, a tapestry of people and ecosystems intertwined into a complex socioecological system.

I inhale the smell of sawdust and chafed earth, the ridge top bleeding in the sunlight. This driveway, this house, is just one more tiny cut in the body of this biosphere, just one more freedom taken from this living world. The people who own this land have chosen to create a better life for themselves, to build a secret and personal oasis. This will be a remote and beautiful home for their family, a place where they will raise healthy, curious children. They have grasped their freedom and chosen to make their lives better.

Down in the valley, thousands of people with their own children are held in the womb of these mountains, their lives supported in countless ways by the forests rising around them. Now, they look up to the ridge, this hole in the forest, the place where a single family has improved their lives at the expense of their connected ecological and human community. They watch the sunlight shine off this house's new windows, their eyes drawn to this monument to power and privilege and individual freedom.

The people of the valley cannot afford to own their own land, to build and maintain a mile-long driveway, to construct a new house on the ridge, but their freedom is tied to the freedom of the people who can. In the forest of our world, some acorns land in the deep soils of the floodplains; others wedge into cracks in the rocks. Freedom is not apportioned equally, is not democratic, not diverse, not representative. The trees of the privileged soar easily into the canopy, experiencing a radical and boundless freedom. The rest of the world lives in their shade.

I look west, to where Johnnie Brook ripples around the base of Chamberlain Hill, running to join the waters of the big river. I wonder who could resist this place—this community, these forests, these waters. People flow to the broad valley like streams to a river, each seeking a life of beauty and prosperity and purpose. As they come, they build houses and driveways, turn fields and forests into houses and lawns of cut grass, divide the remaining expanses of forest into smaller and smaller pieces. Each person is innocent: a winter tick on the flank of a moose, taking just one small share of the sweetness of the world. Each wonders how a tithe so small could injure something so massive and so boundless and so vital. Slowly, and with good intent, they kill the thing that they love.

The driveway and the house on the ridge have changed this forest forever. It has changed the way that wildlife travels across the mountain, has disrupted their ability to move between habitats at different times and for different purposes, to access new habitats as our climate changes. It has precluded species that only live in expanses of unbroken forest, inciting a panoply of *edge* effects: an array of stressors and ecological impacts that emanate from driveways, house sites, and other edges and extend hundreds of feet into the forest. As small as they may seem, the choices made by these landowners, and by countless others like them, have implications for thousands of species of living things, for peoples across this world, for countless future generations. As we turn our heads in deference to each landowner's individual freedom, this action is repeated again and again across the broad valley and the valleys beyond.

I watch the wind rake the ridge, raising clouds of dust. A few miles from here, the trees in Bear Island's forest inhale carbon dioxide, storing it in their trunks and in the deepening soils at their feet, exhaling oxygen into the clear air. Bear Island Brook and Berta Brook filter clean, cold water into the Winooski River, flowing through the broad valley below. Bear

Island's forest provides habitat for wildlife from white-tailed deer to neotropical songbirds, from bees to ants to butterflies. Bear Island produces firewood and lumber: local, renewable resources that provide warmth, shelter and economic opportunity for my neighbors and my community. The benefits that Bear Island's forest provides are not luxuries to be enjoyed by a lucky few. They are necessities: the ecological, cultural, and economic foundation of this society and the freedom of its people. They do not belong to me—they belong to all of us, and they belong to our children.

With my freedom, I could develop Bear Island, could fragment it with driveways and houses, could cut its timber and mine its gravel, could break it into pieces and exploit its finite resources. With my freedom, I could become rich and comfortable, could make my life easy, could put food in my children's mouths and money in their pockets, could turn the forest on the mountain into a source of wealth and power for my family for generations. I was born in the rich soils of the valley, destined to tower, fated to be free. I wonder what it would mean to use my freedom and my power to embody something different.

I place a hand on the rough bark of a wolf tree, feeling it shiver in the wind. Each of its twisting branches reach toward the light. Each can only grow, can only find freedom, within the structure of the tree—an entity that belongs to all its branches and to none of them. I wonder if we could learn to see our dreams and our freedoms within a collective dream, a collective freedom. Could we learn to see freedom as a responsibility as much as a right? Could we learn to see that the true purpose of freedom is not to enrich ourselves but to care for this living world and to care for each other?

Life is so bittersweet. Below me, the forests of the broad valley reach out to each other across stone walls and wire fences, over roads and houses, through the air and the soil, through the bodies of the animals that pass between them. This mountain and this valley are connected to the mountains and the valleys beyond, drawn together across space and time.

The shape of this moment breaks over me like the waves of a vast ocean, filling my nostrils with salt spray. From the naked ridge top, I feel summer drawing its last breaths. The birds are flying south, the westerly wind turning the leaves of the trees. I look out over the broad valley, a living world ringing with the bells of change.

The sun rises over *Moziozagan*, the moosehump mountain. It is summer in Vermont and the air is as thick and as sweet as honey, rolling through the truck's open windows. I wind through a forest of sugar maple and yellow birch and beech, their leaves still wet with dew.

The road ends at a frayed clearing, an ancient house hunched at its center. The clearing is fringed with rusted farm equipment, gutted cars, a half-rotted pole barn stuffed with bags of trash and piles of scrap steel. A sugar maple wolf tree leans beside the house's faded front door. Acres of freshly mown hayfields glitter behind.

In the morning light, the house is the ghost of something old and beautiful. Centuries ago, this house was built with pride and purpose, trimmed with elaborate decoration. It stood along a road between two bustling villages, planted on a sprawling farm of pastures and orchards, hayfields and cropland, a paradise of space and soil. The house was a vision of hope and prosperity and freedom.

Today, the house leans into the wind, three stories of chipping paint and rotting shutters. Today, the lives of the people who built this house are myths, as forgotten as the ancient forests that they once cleared. Only the house remembers the aching bodies and the hardened hands, the generations of birth and death, joy and struggle. Only the house remembers the apples in the cellar and the butter in the churn, the eggs frying as children swung their legs at the kitchen table, the horses in the barn whickering into their oats.

Through the wavy glass of the house's windows, I can see stacks of yellow newspapers, counters and windowsills crowded with dusty trash. The pastures and orchards and the cropland that fed the house's children, that made its owners rich, are gone. The county is full of farms like this: the legacies of a lost past, like signs pointing to nowhere. Wealth now blooms in the county from more distant things.

This morning, I drove east on the state highway, passing through sprawling neighborhoods of single-family homes where once were fields and forests. Each year the bulldozers and the excavators, the cranes and cement mixers, reach outward from the center of the county. Each year they crawl further toward its edges, further up its slopes, deeper into its forest blocks. Each year, the human world expands and the forest retracts, pressed further to the margins.

As I passed through endless acres of bright new homes, the old farmhouses were rotten teeth in a white smile, tractors rusting in their dooryards. The neighborhoods were dark; only the windows of the farmhouses were alight, glowing yellow in the dawn. The matriarchs and patriarchs of the old farm families sat at their kitchen tables, cradling cups of coffee in their scarred hands.

Decades ago, the state highway would have carried me through a world of dairy farms, the lights in their long barns glowing. Decades ago, the morning milking done, the farmers would have been leading herds of bony cattle through rocky pastures, kicking up whistling woodcocks. Today, the old-timers' coffee is lightened with milk from farms far away. Today, the pastures are colonies of identical houses, robed with vinyl siding and asphalt shingles. The hay meadows are long, flat strip malls that could be anywhere in America.

Jack waits for me on the old house's porch, its gray planks fading downward to one corner. He is a man in late middle age, his short beard marbled with silver, his calloused hands tucked into the pockets of a pair of faded blue jeans.

I am a service forester; my job is to advise private landowners like Jack on how to care for their forests. Though Jack called me here to walk through his woodlot, he seems surprised and amused as I approach him—with my new orange vest, my unwrinkled face, my arms decorated with tattoos. The corners of his eyes wrinkle under the frayed bill of his baseball cap as I climb the porch steps. As I often do in the presence of old-timers, I feel as young and as shiny and as shallow as a new house in an ancient pasture.

The house creaks behind us as we introduce ourselves and make small talk. I learn that Jack is a mechanic by trade, the youngest son of the family that has owned this house and this land for generations. He tells me that his family's farm once stretched clear back to the old town road but has been shrinking for a century, parts and pieces sold off over the years to make ends meet. The corners of his mouth turn slightly upward. He tells me has been managing the farm's woodlot for the last thirty years without help or guidance, simply doing what felt right.

As the day brightens, Jack and I cross the hayfields, following a narrow, well-maintained tractor trail into the woods. The trail curls around outcrops of sand-colored dolostone, its cracks and soft edges laced with tendrils of moss. We walk through a young forest of basswood, sugar maple, white ash, and bitternut hickory, a single generation of trees with trunks just large enough to wrap two hands around. I can tell that where we walk was a cow pasture sixty years ago, that like many others it was abandoned in the 1950s or 1960s.

Though this forest is just beginning its journey through time, richness hides in every crevice, greenness filling every space. The understory is thick with maidenhair fern, blue cohosh, Virginia waterleaf, and seersucker sedge, the plants of sweet, calcium-rich soils. I can tell that in spring the forest floor will be a carpet of wild leeks, their twin leaves like rabbits' ears, and this forest will smell of garlic.

Since he was a young man, Jack has managed this forest for firewood, the dozen cords a year needed to heat the leaky old house. If he wished, he could have simply cut all the biggest trees, could have taken from the forest with carelessness. Instead, he has tended this forest like a garden: weeding around each of its healthiest trees, cutting less-healthy trees and giving those with the most promise room to grow. His work has not been in vain: the trail passes through acres of young, vigorous hardwood trees, each with tight, beautiful bark, each with a dense, well-balanced crown.

Though Jack's forest is hopeful, it echoes with scars. Like Bear Island, like nearly every forest that I visit, this forest has been pounded like an anvil; cleared and farmed and exploited, its sweetness sapped, its treasures pulled like stones from the soil. In living their dreams of individual freedom, past generations garnished this land's riches, enriching themselves with a piece of Jack's freedom. Because of the choices of his ancestors, Jack will weed this garden for the rest of his life without ever seeing an abundant harvest, without ever seeing this forest truly become itself. He will spend his life raising this child, and he will never see it truly live.

It is a common story: yesterday's freedom taken at the expense of today's. Because of the freedoms of past generations, my generation has never had the freedom to live among healthy, diverse forests; a stable climate and a thriving biosphere; wolves and catamounts, elk and passenger pigeons; ancient, unbroken landscapes and clear, boundless waters. Because of the opulence and the carelessness of the past, we must find freedom within a climate crisis and a biodiversity crisis, a mass extinction, within degraded and fragmented ecosystems facing an uncertain future. We have been born into a reality in which each generation takes their freedom from the same shrinking and finite pool. We have been told that we are radically free—and then handed a world in which each generation is less free than the last.

I feel a kinship with Jack. Across the hayfield, the old house teeters and falls apart, empty cans pressed against the glass. The forest around us is young and simple, missing so many of the things that once defined it. Jack did not choose this forest, this land, this old house. Both are legacies—things that simply are what they are. With his freedom as a landowner, Jack could have chosen to exploit this forest, to subdivide and develop this land. He could have used the money he earned to retire, to build a new house in place of the old. Instead, he has taken a different path. As I have at Bear Island, Jack has chosen to pick up the pieces that remain and to try to build something beautiful.

I marvel at Jack's forest, this profound expression of care and compassion in a world of exploitation and short-sightedness. Jack has no children, no one that he is managing this forest for. He is simply building a better legacy for those who may some-day follow, whoever they are. He has cared for this forest not because he had to but because he has chosen to—because he is called toward responsibility. Like each of us, Jack has a house to keep and a forest to tend; a life of his own and a life to give to the world. Like each of us, Jack must find a way to care for the garden of his imperfect life while tending to the garden that we all share.

Freedom is a chainsaw, with the potential to be so many good and terrible things. We cannot choose if we will cut into the flesh of this biosphere, cannot choose whether or not our freedom will impact the freedom of others and of future generations. All that we can do is choose how we will live in the world that we have been given: if we will treat this earth like a mine or a garden, if we will exploit and abuse it or if we will turn toward relationship and responsibility and find a way to live with compassion.

We walk back through the hayfield and toward the old house, its clapboards bobbing in a sea of goldenrod. As Jack and I chat, I am brimming with hope. Suddenly, I can imagine finding balance in this off-kilter world. I can envision a reality where enriching each other is as important as enriching ourselves, where freedom is something that we can only attain together. This morning, I can envision a world where we see our power and our freedom as tools to plant seeds in the earth: to offer future generations a freedom unknown to the world of today.

We draw out our goodbyes, lingering in the shade of Jack's ancient sugar maple, watching breezes comb the tall grasses of the dooryard. As we talk, Jack squints toward the treeline, the forest where he has spent his life working like a gardener with his hands in the soil.

In the morning light, the old-timers sit at their kitchen tables, their nostalgia thick and bittersweet. They reminisce, mourning the fact that their children and grandchildren will never drive cattle through the rocky pasture, that future generations will never know the world of their childhood. As they linger in the past, I look toward the future, hoping that their grandchildren will know a different meaning of the word freedom.

We are leaving Virginia, leaving the hotel and the box stores, their parking lots still crowded with cars and people. I turn the Camry back onto the highway and point toward home. As we travel north, we fall back in time: the forest blocks get bigger, the development and the deer and the invasive plants receding. After many long hours, we enter the broad valley at dusk. I see the crooked ridge of Stimson Mountain, silhouetted again by a pink sky.

In the morning I rush to Bear Island, wondering what plants are in flower, what tracks and trails have been etched in the sandy soil, what beautiful things have transpired in my brief absence. I know that there has never been, and will never be, a moment like this one. The future of the world is being written, and I want to wander its pages.

Soon I stand on a cloud, kneeling on the edge of a cliff. The crowns of oaks stir the mist, their roots anchored in soils gathered far below. Around me, the lichen-coated rocks are islands in an ocean of fog, the bones of the mountain pressing through its breathing skin. In the eyes of the human world, Bear Island is my "property"—something I own, an object that I possess. The forest around me defies such a definition. Bear Island spreads in every direction, its ledges cloaked with trees and the soft bodies of plants, a city of trillions engaged in the practice of life.

I watch the cars travel the twin lanes of the highway, gone in five seconds. Inside each are people living complex lives: seeking happiness, purpose, and freedom. I wonder what this world would become if they could see, just for five seconds, that we are branches on the same tree, trees in the same forest. I wonder what this world would become if we realized that freedom does not belong to us—that it is borrowed from this living world, borrowed from those without freedom, borrowed from the world of the future. I wonder if we could learn to seek individual freedom within collective freedom, individual liberation within collective liberation, individual prosperity within collective prosperity. I imagine, in this epoch of loneliness, what would happen if we reached toward freedom together.

Beneath my feet, the reindeer moss is a reef of lacing complexity, painted on the rocks. Through it, a pink *Corydalis* blooms. Like each of us, like the world we inhabit, the Corydalis is a strange and lovely little flower. She blooms from the ledge's narrow fissures, reminding me that true freedom is to have enough and to be a small part of something beautiful.

In a few months I will sign the papers. I will donate a conservation easement on this land, giving away the freedom to destroy it, to mine it, to subdivide it, to develop it, forever. With my freedom I will choose to protect this place on behalf of countless people, countless living things, countless future generations. I will use my power to give my power away, use my wealth to make everyone rich, give up a piece of my freedom so that everyone will be a little more free.

Conserving my land will never make economic sense, will never be understood by people who see freedom as something to be taken rather than something to be shared. The people on the highway will shake their heads—let them. I reach for the courage to sing a different song and hope to find harmony amid the dissonance of this modern world. It is a dream as subversive and as beautiful as the Corydalis, blooming from the cracks in the rock.

It is in moments like this that the ghosts of the future visit me. Everything everywhere reaches toward freedom, each life as precious as my own. A hermit thrush sings its resonant song, and I am filled with a vision of hope for a better world.

7 | RELATIONSHIP: THE DOE HUNTER

The air is cool and clear, the moon casting backward shadows through the forest. I wait for the light, sipping coffee in my tree stand in the forked oak, feeling like a bear in a tree. I watch the shadows of leaves drift in front of me as the stars fade, as the sky turns from black to blue to purple.

It is early October, and summer is gone. The sun arrives later in the morning and leaves earlier in the evening, the eyelids of the world opening more slowly each day. While the oaks' leaves remain steadfastly green, the sugar maples have turned yellow and orange, layering the forest floor in scattered gold.

Over the last weeks, I have witnessed this forest on its ponderous trek through time. Morning after morning I have awakened in darkness and driven to this lakeside forest to sit in the forked oak. I have seen summer slowly ebb away, pulled southward like a tide over the sand, seen the icy tendrils of winter begin to touch the land. I see it all from fifteen feet above the ground, my eyes aching from watching.

In the cedar swamp the deer are troops in a bunker, their brown eyes blinking through barricades of fallen trees. They wait through the heat of the day, tall ears swiveling, surrounded by mossy booby traps of sound. They cannot wait forever. At dusk, they leave their enclave and move nakedly up the hill, newly fallen leaves soft beneath their hooves.

As the people of the world stack their firewood, fill their oil tanks, and stock their freezers, the deer armor themselves for the starvation of winter. Unlike the people, they have no freezers and no pantries, no endless supermarkets. Unlike the squirrels, they have no secret caches of acorns in the leaves. As winter approaches they must store the apples and the acorns of autumn in their swelling bodies, under their thickening coats. In December, the acorns will be gone. The deer will nip twigs and buds through the snow, their bodies dwindling like my firewood pile— hoping to last until May.

The light rises, and the highway drones distantly over the gentle sounds of the waking forest. As I sit in the forked oak, the highway carries the people of the world through the shifting sands of the Anthropocene; human influence touches the tallest mountain and the deepest ocean, the white sands of every desert, the curling tendrils of the densest jungle. As forests blur in their windshields, the people inhabit a biosphere in the midst of a biodiversity crisis, a mass extinction in which thousands, or perhaps hundreds of thousands, of species have vanished. The people inhabit a planet lurching through a climate crisis that will change their lives, the ecosystems they rely on, and the lives of the species that comprise those ecosystems, forever. The people on the highway pass through ecosystems built on human legacies too numerous to count, through a world that is changed and changing, human and wild, ancient and new.

I begin to see the shapes of familiar things: my crossbow, my backpack, the tether that links me to the forked oak, the shining carabiner that links me to my tether. Soon I can see the profiles of red cedars and white cedars, their boughs like green lace. In this forest, the cedars are pioneers: the trees that reclaimed a rocky, lakeside pasture and transformed it into forest again. Now they are dying, their lower branches curling skyward like bleached bones. Their role fulfilled, they fade slowly into obsolesce. Between them, the whitewashed trunks of sugar maple ascend through the windows in the breaking canopy.

As the forest opens to my eyes, I feel briefly artificial—I am an intruder, a splinter in the flesh of this place. I am wrapped in camouflage, its fabric spun from oil pulled from the body of this earth, a substance with the power to poison soil and water and human bodies, a substance that has driven nations to war. Beneath the camouflage is my wool sweater, woven from fiber grown on the backs of sheep in some faraway pasture—a forest in exile, as this forest once was. The dawn light shines off my crossbow, its metal smelted from ore mined on some distant continent, pulled from a hole in the ground where no forest will ever grow again. As I watch dawn crest over the land, my body soft and warm, an invisible thread ties me to the oil well, the pasture, the mine. They are all a part of me.

I shift in my harness, listening to the rustling of my body. Even as we hold them at arm's length, the relationship between humans and ecosystems is pervasive, defying the apparent distance between us. As people awaken in the highest tower of the most steel-clad metropolis, oxygen from trees and plants fills their lungs. As people live their buzzing modern lives, their bodies are fueled by carbon pulled from the air by living plants, by fruits and vegetables pollinated by native insects, by rainclouds seeded by trees, by the biological communities that infuse the living soil.

As we change our climate and our ecosystems, we learn how vulnerable we are to the vagaries of climate and weather, to rain and drought, to an array of natural phenomena that we can influence but not control. We learn how subtle shifts in this biosphere can manifest natural disasters, famine, disease and war, the loss of the cultures and the livelihoods of entire peoples. It is inescapable: each of us is tethered to a biosphere that has changed on a scale and in a timeframe unknown to the annals of history and that changes more profoundly each day. Each of us relies on it for every breath. We cannot live without it.

A loon's call echoes over the lake. I watch the woods awaken. This biosphere, this planet, is a miracle, a gift of abundance. It is neither replaceable nor infinite nor immortal.

Orange strands of sunlight crest the Green Mountains, touching my face. I blink and shadows have become shapes, shapes becoming the familiar contours of the forest. I see the cracked mounds of dolostone, the cedars huddled in the swamp, the twisted strands of a split-rail fence laid by some farmer sweating on this hillside a century ago. As the light blooms in the forest, I see the sugar maple seedlings, twisted and stunted from deer browse, the nonnative invasive buckthorn and honeysuckle, the yellow grass growing where a generation of young trees should be.

The forest stirs. The squirrels move first, racing through the leaves in bursts of shuffling sound. Soon, a scurrying drama is unfolding; squirrels are gathering and caching acorns, chasing and chattering at one another. A barred owl hoots, and they are quiet for a moment before resuming their chores.

This forest is a volume of relationships, too numerous to count. Within it every creature, every plant, every insect, every tree affects one another, changing the shape of this community in some small way. Like every ecosystem on earth, this forest is a study in *symbiosis*—the many imperfect ways that living things build themselves of each other, the many crooked shapes and shades of community. While symbiosis is often confused with mutualism—a mutually beneficial relationship between organisms—the term actually refers to *any* close relationship between organisms. The forms of symbiosis include mutualism and also *commensalism* (a relationship where one creature benefits and the other is unaffected), *parasitism*, *predation*, and *competition*.

As comforting as it would be to believe that this forest is a community built entirely on mutualism, the reality of symbiosis is far more expansive and powerful. This forest is as tough as nails and delicate as silk, a community sustained by death as much as by life. The relationships between its pieces and parts are as peaceful as trees and mycorrhizal fungi and as jarring as predators and prey, parasites and hosts. Within this living system, organisms communicate and collaborate and also compete with one another, kill one another, destroy one another's habitat; at least one-third of the species on earth are considered parasites. It is not for us to judge the quality of these relationships, to decide that one form of symbiosis is better than any other. It is up to us to reimagine forests: to learn that forests are beautiful because of what they are, not what we wish them to be.

I scan the woods, my eyes picking apart the spaces between the trees. I am not here just to watch. I am here for a purpose, to prosecute a strange and tender part of my relationship—my symbiosis—with this forest. I am here to take the life of a living thing, a deer that was once a fawn, born in the soft grasses of spring, standing shakily in her damp, spotted coat. I am here to kill a deer that has passed a winter or two in the cedars, raised in the sirens and the silences of this modern world.

The light breaks the dam of the mountains and pours over the forest like a flood, turning everything to pink and gold. When hunting season is over, I will forget the bitter cold, the long spans of boredom, the failures and frustrations. I will cradle my coffee in front of the wood stove and think only of moments like this: the forest illuminated in the first light of morning, the owl wing-beats on my face, the gaggle of does ambling just out of range, the hawks hunting like dancers, six inches off the ground.

In Vermont, precolonial populations of white-tailed deer were likely small—limited to the warmer valleys by harsh winters, predation, and competition from other large ungulates. Three centuries ago, wolves and eastern cougars (catamounts) roamed this forest, hunting deer, moose, elk, and caribou. On this morning, the eastern elk are extinct, the caribou gone. The wolves and the cougars have been lost from this forest for centuries, their habitat decimated, hunted and bountied to extinction.

In his essay *Thinking Like a Mountain*, written in 1944, Aldo Leopold reflected on killing a wolf:

> I thought that fewer wolves meant more deer, and that more deer meant hunter's paradise. But after seeing the

green fire [in the wolf's eyes] die, I sensed that neither the wolf nor the mountain agreed with such a view.

Since then I have lived to see state after state extirpate its wolves. I have watched the face of many a newly wolfless mountain, and seen the south-facing slopes wrinkle with a maze of new deer trails. I have seen every edible bush and seedling browsed, first to anaemic desuetude, and then to death. I have seen every edible tree defoliated to the height of a saddlehorn. Such a mountain looks as if someone had given God a new pruning shears, and forbidden Him all other exercise. In the end the starved bones of the hoped-for deer herd, dead of its own too-much, bleach with the bones of the dead sage, or molder under the high-lined junipers.

I now suspect that just as a deer herd lives in mortal fear of its wolves, so does a mountain live in mortal fear of its deer.

I watch a nuthatch climb the bark of a cedar. Like many other species, deer were nearly or completely driven out of Vermont in the 1800s. Like a chosen few, deer were reintroduced: a small herd was released into the state in 1878. The people of the time could not have known how the deer would respond to the loss of predation and competition, to less severe winters, to the young forests that regenerated from the abandoned pastures of the 1900s, to the increasingly fragmented and suburbanized landscape that followed. It was beyond imagining that deer could ever degrade a forest.

Today, deer are overpopulated throughout much of the United States, a major threat to biodiversity and ecological integrity across nearly an entire continent. Through the innocent act of grazing plants and browsing young trees, deer can make things that they prefer to eat—from ginseng to oaks to orchids— scarce, and things that they avoid—like nonnative invasive plants and beech—abundant. While some browsing and grazing is normal, too many deer and too much browsing can manifest profound and pervasive changes in forests. At a time when forests' best hope for the future lies in diversity, adaptability, and resilience, too much deer browse makes forests less diverse, less adaptable, and less resilient; it encourages infestations of nonnative invasive plants and degrades habitat for other wildlife species, from bears to butterflies. In its most extreme iteration, deer browse can drive a process known as *forest disintegration*, where the regeneration of the forest halts entirely.

Like us, deer are guilty of their own "too much," a jolting cog in this soft machine. Like us, their lives come at a cost. Like us, they degrade the world that gives them life, flourishing at the expense of the ecosystems that they inhabit.

I listen to the drumming highway, watching squirrels bound through the understory, watching sugar maple leaves settle on the forest floor. My mind sinks under waves of spiraling, meaningless thoughts, adrift and unraveling, wandering through a landscape without edges or boundaries or corners.

A form separates from the shadows of the forest—a slender leg, a long body—and everything comes into focus. Suddenly, the lines of the forest are sharp in my eyes, its colors bright and piercing, its every sound distinct. Another form follows the first, and another. Three does are returning to the swamp, idling in the embers of dawn. They step softly in their fall coats, bending, chewing, preening. One edges forward, and I raise my crossbow.

Twenty years ago, I walked up a gravel road with my brother and my friends, through the cornfields and past the pond. We sat at scratched desks in a makeshift basement classroom, learning the rules and the ethics of hunting. I remember that the air was suffused with the smells of gun oil, dampness, and mildew, the dusty shelves crowded with antlers and taxidermied animals.

The next October, I hunted with my father along Leach Brook, the smooth stock of a rifle heavy in my child's hands. I do not remember what I felt in my first moments and days as a hunter: if I was scared or brave, harsh or tender. I do not remember what I believed that I was hunting for, or what thoughts or feelings carried me into the woods. As I trace my fragments of memory, what I remember most clearly is the long-haired coyote, cresting the narrow ridge and catching us in her yellow eyes.

In my adolescence, I stopped hunting and pursued other things. I searched for meaning and for trouble, traveled and explored. It was not until I became a forester until I saw the pervasive and troubling impacts of deer on forests, that I picked up my old rifle and became a hunter again.

A flock of Canada geese flies noisily overhead, an arrow pointing south. My heart pounds as the deer scrape the leaves with their pointed hooves, the fine hairs on their black noses brushing the soil. The doe's head bobs, her body still hidden by brush. I struggle to control my breathing, to keep my hands steady, to wait for my shot.

The north wind gusts, carrying the does' scent to me. Somewhere, the bone-crowned bucks are beginning to twitch, their heads raised, sniffing the autumn air. Soon, they will become wary and territorial, will run themselves ragged looking for mates, fighting each other, rubbing and scraping and hooking trees with their antlers, tilting with windmills. They will push clusters of does through the forest, hounding them for days on the chance that one might come into heat.

Soon, the other hunters will come to the forest with their rifles, searching for the biggest, the heaviest, the largest-antlered buck on every mountain. I can hear them now, their brash voices carrying over the clatter of the diner. The hunters are bucks in their own right, rutting in the woods. To them, hunting is a game and deer are a prize to be taken, a badge of honor to be seized with a bullet. When they find their quarry, they will pull the trigger without hesitation.

I was in my early twenties when I began hunting again, a young forester, eager to prove myself. The foresters and the loggers that I worked with were masks of masculinity and competence, hard and impenetrable and impervious. Each was a hunter, a farmer, a diesel mechanic; each knew how to fix a tractor and build a house and slaughter a pig. Next to them, I felt helpless and useless and small. I hungered for their respect and their approval.

During this time, I discovered that I possessed a superpower: a relentlessness, an insatiable tenacity. I could work endlessly without eating or drinking or resting, could lose hours in a task before surfacing, gasping, wondering where I had gone. I began to identify this relentlessness as a different aspect of my personality, a piece of myself that I called Spud. While Ethan was soft and tender and uncertain, Spud was ruthless and unfeeling, impervious to exhaustion and fatigue, unwilling to tolerate weakness or failure. As Spud, there was no beauty in my work, no beauty in the forest; all that existed was the next tree to be marked, the next hill to climb, the next step to take, the next benchmark to achieve. I became a machine of competence, productivity, and efficiency, and was rewarded with success and respect and recognition.

Even as I found success as a forester, I continued to fail as a hunter. I spent years waiting for a buck in the drifting snow, ending each season empty-handed. The more frustrated I became, the more Spud infused my hunting. I became as driven and as single-minded as a rangy young wolf; I could not let a morning in deer season pass without sitting under the frozen hemlocks, could not leave the woods until it was enveloped in darkness. I hungered for a buck, my bloodshot eyes raking the contours of the autumn forest, my gloved hands clenching the stock of my rifle. By December, I was a buck after the rut: broken and exhausted, as thin and as tough as old leather. I would lay down the rifle and rejoin my herd in its war of attrition against the deep, white winter, my hands empty again.

The doe pauses in the circle of my scope, bathed in light. She is beautiful and vital, a living being navigating an elaborate world of her own. My finger tightens against the smooth metal of the crossbow's trigger, and I wonder what a wolf feels in the moments before a kill. The autumn air presses like a ghost against my cheek.

As I watch the doe, I feel no ambition, no hunger. Spud simmers somewhere deep in the caverns of my mind, his edges softened, one of the many pieces of a complex identity. Today, I am less interested in personal glory than I am in protecting forests, less interested in trophies than I am in helping maintain a sustainable population of deer on this landscape. Because a buck can mate with multiple does, killing a buck does little to affect the deer population; lowering the deer population means killing does, an act that many hunters have long considered taboo. I have stopped caring what this world expects of me and tried to become what this world needs.

Autumn has become a time for sitting in a tree, watching the leaves turn their colors. Like most predators, I am rarely successful. Like most predators, my greatest strength is my persistence. I climb the forked oak before dawn, day after day, spending mornings listening to leaves settling on the ground, watching the wings of blue jays flash through the trees. Some days I see deer and some days I do not. No day is a failure.

The doe takes a half-step forward, the morning light shining over her long neck. I think of the people who would pull the trigger without a thought and the people who would let a deer live, regardless of the cost. I have learned that neither of these paths is enough, that both are missing something. Even as deer threaten the forests that I love, I have learned there is room enough inside of me for both action and compassion. I have learned that I can love deer and kill deer, love trees and cut trees, and that to do so can be an act of humility and profound responsibility.

My hands tighten around the stock of the crossbow. I watch the doe feed, her short tail flicking idly. In the valleys of the human world, forests are cleared, wetlands drained, mountains removed, ecosystems destroyed to keep people happy and healthy and safe. The earth shudders in the midst of a mass extinction—the sixth such event in the known history of our planet, the first caused by a single species. Everywhere, ecosystems teeter on the brink of collapse, the climate changing faster than they can adapt. Everywhere, oil spreads through salt water like a toxic shadow, the air is infused with poison, rivers ignite, human bodies bloom with cancers. Racism, inequity, and injustice smolder in our communities, dictating a person's opportunity to breathe clean air, to drink clean water, to live full and fruitful lives.

Like every creature and every person on earth, I will always have a relationship with ecosystems, will always touch them, will always change them, will always take from them to survive. Unlike the deer, I have the power and the freedom to choose what the shape of my relationship with this world will be. In moments like this, the profound choices necessary to save what is precious are naked in my eyes.

As the hunters of Vermont age and retire, I imagine future generations of hunters like me, who hunt not for bigger bucks and more deer but for a sustainable population of deer on the landscape. As the loggers of Vermont age and retire, I imagine future generations of loggers like me, who cut trees so that forests will be healthy and diverse and resilient, a richer legacy for future generations.

I am the doe hunter, to whom hunting is an act of humility and an act of love. I am the doe hunter, who sees beauty in a living deer and a dead deer, in living trees and trees stacked on the log landing, ready to be sent to the mill. I am the doe hunter, choosing complexity over simplicity, responsibility over comfort. I am the doe hunter, a brave and imperfect being in a world of nuance. I am the doe hunter. Like this world, I am many things at once.

My crossbow clatters against the trunk of the forked oak. The doe looks up, her blue-veined ears swiveling, her eyes scanning the understory. After a long moment, she gives herself a little shake and settles back into the serious work of puttering around, searching for acorns.

The doe inches ahead. The blood pounds in my ears. I feel a tug in my chest, my body tense, my mind wondering, "Is this right? Is this right?" The doe dips her elegant neck. My gaze lingers over her shoulder, where her lungs fill with the same air that I now breathe, where her heart fills with warm red blood, just like mine. Like myself, like the trees in this forest, the doe is a part of an expansive reality, a creature who has done nothing wrong but to be born into this tattered world. Part of me wants her to live, to thrive, to get old and fat, to mother countless spotted fawns, but I know that it cannot be. Like the death of a tree, I know that the death of a deer can be a gift to the other creatures of the forest. I know that the death of this beautiful animal can mean habitat and refuge, abundance and resilience for countless living things, an ecosystem brought back into balance.

I pull the trigger and the cable snaps. The doe springs away, her tail tucked between her legs. I watch as she zigs and zags, unsure which way to run, cradling her life like water in a basket— something she cannot hold, but that she must. Her sisters lift their long necks as she dives into the swamp, the morning woods swallowing her.

I am engulfed in static, silence burning in my ears. The other does finish chewing and turn, weaving like dancers into the tangle of fallen cedar. As my chest heaves, I see the shapes of their bodies as they dawdle in shadows of the swamp, pawing the earth. After a long moment they wander away, their outlines merging and fading.

I try to calm myself, my hands shaking, my chest pounding. Around me, the forest pulses gently, no different than a moment ago. The squirrels continue their gathering and chasing. The nuthatches flit up and down the bark of a white oak, picking at things too small to see. The sun filters through the maple leaves. Only the doe, and I, have changed.

I wait as long as I can, suspended in time. After many thunderous minutes, I descend the forked oak with stumbling hands. Twenty yards away, my arrow angles from the leaves like a beacon, streaked with red. I kneel and hold it in my hands, the doe's blood cooling on my fingertips. I stand and see the white flag of her tail, resting on the leaves.

I watch the doe's still body, so deeply sorry that things need to be this way. I can no longer choose not to choose, decide not to decide; a better world calls to me, and I am thrust into relationship. I believe that the future belongs to people with the courage and the compassion to do what is necessary, even when it breaks their hearts.

The doe lays across the earth, green fans of cedar all around her. The skin of her neck gathers in small, glowing folds, her eyelashes long and dark and curled.

I stay there for a while, my hand resting on her warm flank. What a strange world we live in, I think, her body soft under my fingertips. How hard it is to do something truly good.

8 | HUMILITY: THE LOGGERS

The sound echoes off the sides of the valley, a whirring, screaming drone. The feller-buncher moves through the forest like a giant yellow spider, its steel mandibles reaching for a diseased beech tree, grasping and severing it in a single motion.

A grapple-skidder roars up the trail, wraps its hydraulic claws around a pile of trees and drags it away, the treetops tracing lines in the dust. The action is repeated, again and again. From above, the skidders are ants at a picnic, tracing and retracing their steps to some sugary treasure.

The feller-buncher's saw whines, its pitch lowering as it tears through column after column of living wood. With each cut the clearing widens, the massive machine pushing back the walls of the forest. Behind it, the skid trail curls through the patch cut like the trunk of an ancient oak, splitting and branching, stacks of felled trees feathering it like leaves. Like a greedy child, the feller-buncher reaches for another tree and another, gathering flowers into a giant bouquet.

It is August, 2017. Only one month ago, I became the owner of this land, and already I am changing it forever. I watch the machines work with my heart in my throat, wondering if I am doing the right thing.

Two weeks earlier I climbed the main skid trail, my orange vest packed with florescent flagging tape and tree marking paint, my paint gun bumping against my thigh. It was a familiar beginning to a day in the woods. For years, I worked as a consulting forester on private lands in Vermont, New Hampshire and Maine. Countless mornings began just like this: with a walk down some old skid trail, the weight of a gallon of tree-marking paint tugging at my shoulders, my paint gun at my side.

Being a consulting forester was empowering and also lonely; each day, I would wake at dawn and drive to some remote forest, my dog JR sleeping in the cab behind me. In the heat of summer, in pouring rain, in the snows of winter, JR and I would walk endless miles—marking trees to be cut, supervising loggers, gathering data for forest management plans. At the end of each day I would return, exhausted, to my shared house in Burlington. As I walked up the driveway, music would be playing, the windows of the yellow house illuminated in the blue light of dusk. My roommates would be talking and joking, cooking dinner, having lived days of city lives. JR and I would enter like aliens from some distant planet, our legs weak and our shoulders hunched, speckled with blue tree-marking paint. On many days the first words I said would be then—when I got home in the evening.

I felt the weight of my paint gun, its trigger tucked into my pants' pocket. Consulting foresters do many things, but what I remember most vividly are the days marking trees to be cut, the bittersweet feeling of sentencing another tree to death with every pull of the paint gun's orange trigger. I do not know how many trees I have marked in my young life—tens, perhaps hundreds, of thousands. When I began my career as a consulting forester, each tree was a bitter sacrifice, an unspeakable loss, a dagger to my heart. The more time I spent in the woods, the more I understood the nuanced reality of life and death in the forest. I came to understand that each tree was a pixel in a photograph, a tiny piece of a forest community with its own life to live, a world of billions of creatures that reach toward the future together. I learned that the cutting of a tree can be an act of responsibility, an expression of compassion. I learned that the death of a tree is a small price to pay to help a community move forward with grace.

I hooked my middle finger under the paint gun's worn plastic trigger, a gesture as familiar as a hand in a pocket. I had held the paint gun this way as I traversed countless mountains and valleys, crossed rivers and swamps, as I learned what it means to be a forester and as I learned what kind of forester I wanted to be. Beneath the paint gun's battered cover, I had replaced nearly all its parts: every spring and piston and gasket, every nut and bolt and bearing. We had been through so much together. And yet, on this morning, the paint gun in my hand felt different than ever before.

A year before, I left my job as a consulting forester and became a service forester, spending more walking in the woods with people than with a paint gun in my hand. It became my job to advise landowners, loggers, and laypeople; to help people understand what it means to love a forest, what it means to be the steward of an ecosystem at this strange and crucial moment in time. Though being a service forester suited me better, a piece of me missed the long days in snowshoes, the cold biting at my cheeks. A piece of me missed a life of silent action, enacting changes in the forest with every pull of the paint gun's trigger.

At the top of the hill, I paused. Ahead, the tongue of an old skid trail lolled across the cliffs. Vireos sang over the sound of running water, and I breathed deeply. Though I had carried the paint gun through thousands of acres of forest, though I had supervised dozens of logging jobs, though I had advised hundreds of landowners, this was not someone else's land, not some distant forest. This was Bear Island—a place I would spend my life protecting, a place that would someday be my home. I felt as uncertain as the first time that I held the paint gun, its cover shiny and new.

Over the last two weeks, I had explored this land like a child in a castle, wandering from room to treasure-filled room. I had found wetlands and waterfalls and moss-capped boulders, oaks hiding in crowds of pockmarked beech. I had found little valleys where the soil was moist and deep, home to secret communities of sugar maple and basswood. I had found bear-scarred red pines threading the cliffs' edges, sweet fern and huckleberry and beaked hazelnut filling the understory at their feet. I had found brooks tumbling over white ledges and dens hidden behind the rocks. Everywhere I walked, the gray bones of the earth pressed through the soil, drawing upward toward the southern wall of Stimson Mountain, where the falcons nest.

I listened to the whistle of a wood peewee, the high, bubbling chatter of a group of cedar waxwings, the *po-ta-to-chip* calls of goldfinches. This land was still a stranger to me. I had not yet seen it in spring or fall or winter, in pouring rain or with limbs bent under heavy snow. I had not yet explored its every pinnacle and hollow, had not yet wandered every node of its sprawling

interstices—its rich and precious spaces between. Still, I felt
that this forest had opened itself to me, this wild and vital thing
becoming close enough to touch. I felt Bear Island winking at
me, beauty shining from under layers of scar tissue, hope glimmering in the rubble. Beneath the legacies of human negligence
and ignorance and greed, I caught glimpses of a world of promise, its eyes like glowing coals.

I began walking again, turning onto the old skid trail—a narrow, faded track cutting across the slope. Today, I walked through
the forest on the mountain with a different purpose: searching
not for treasures but for places that were beyond hope.

The skid trail led me into a stand of diseased beech, a generation
of twisted and stunted trees overtopping a dense sea of clones.
Thirty years earlier this had been a stand of red oak, the beech
creeping up through the understory. Thirty years earlier, loggers
had high-graded the mountain: cutting the oak and releasing the
beech, sending this stand spinning into an endless cycle of beech
growth, decline, and mortality.

I pulled a roll of orange flagging tape from the pocket of my
vest and began marking the perimeter of the beech stand. I had
a plan: inside the orange flagging, I would start over, cutting the
diseased beech trees and their clones, allowing a new generation
of trees to regenerate in their place. By creating larger openings,
I would make the shade-loving beech less competitive, and the
forest would have the chance to reach toward diversity again.
By timing the work for this summer, I would capitalize on a year
when red oak, white pine, red spruce, and sugar maple trees were

all heavy with seed. My plan was sound, and yet I knew that I could only do so much. The forest would have to do the rest.

I moved from tree to tree, marking the edges of the beech stand in orange. My hands remembered the practiced motion—my fingers unrolling, knotting, and tearing the flagging as naturally as a leaf turns toward the sun. Slowly, I marked the boundaries of a patch cut, an acre of trees that would soon be gone.

The air was warm and dry, a perfect July morning. As I encircled the beech stand, I had no desire to dominate this forest, to control it, to force it to conform to some idealized image. More than anything, I wanted the forest on the mountain to be itself: beautiful and wild, free to go its own way. I believed that this forest, its creatures, its patterns and processes, its relationships and connections, had *intrinsic* value—the right to exist. I knew that the best and most vital parts of this living system could not be engineered, that they must create themselves. I also knew that in this moment they needed my help.

Bear Island had been cleared and maintained as a pasture for a century, had been high-graded and exploited in the century that followed. This land had seen the ancient forest and its creatures lost, the oak and all the healthiest trees on the mountain cut, the beech that was once the foundation of its biological community become a different species entirely. Now it was forced to respond to a changing climate, to nonnative pests and pathogens, to deer overpopulation, to countless other iterations and manifestations of global change. This forest was a tender, wounded being, its vitality locked behind the legacies of an unkind past, an impossible present, an uncertain future. Its ancient and delicate living fabric had been twisted and torn, stressed and damaged in unthinkable ways. Its riches had been taken in pieces and in huge, ragged swaths, and I had been handed the broken thing that remained.

As I encircled the patch cut, the forest on the mountain was a swaybacked horse, sickly and beaten and abused, forgotten and suffering in some dirt pasture. I wondered who could believe that it was a greater kindness to do nothing than to do everything possible to help this living thing become healthy again.

I finished marking the patch cut and turned, watching the orange flagging bob in the breeze. As I looked over my work I felt no satisfaction, only the weight of a profound responsibility. Once, it would have been enough to leave this forest alone. Now, to do so would be an act of negligence, a profound abdication of responsibility.

I turned back up the main trail, the silver face of Stimson Mountain looming in the distance. The forest on the mountain was ancient and massive, alive and changing, a community of trillions. In every handful of forest soil, millions or billions of mites, springtails, nematodes, fungi, and bacteria lived out unknowable existences, a universe of tiny creatures under every footstep. Across the mountain, thousands of species of birds, bears, bats, bobcats, weasels, rodents, reptiles, amphibians, and invertebrates inhabited complex and mysterious lives. This was their home.

I traced the shuffling trail of a porcupine around the *talus*— a field of jumbled boulders and rocks gathered at the base of a cliff. Once a part of the cliff, the talus had become a world of its own—a network of caves and dark passages capped with mosses and rockcap polypody. As they fell, the rocks of the talus had left fingerprints on the cliff's face, high ledges where generations of bobcats had watched storms roll through the broad valley. I smiled. In the forest, even something as stoic as this cliff was changing. Like everything in the forest, when it broke it became something new, one thing becoming two becoming many.

I paused, watching the morning light warm the ledges. The cliff face was an ecosystem in its own right, a garden of mosses and blue-gray lichens, red columbine and pink Corydalis glowing from its fissures. I stepped closer, my nose nearly brushing the moist rock. Tiny creatures moved through the moss, navigating a forest in miniature. I knew that a team of scientists could study this cliff for years, teasing apart its intricacies. They could enumerate the cliff's influence on soils, climate, and water, could trace its origin and chart its future. They could parse the biological communities woven around it, all the organisms to whom the cliff is habitat, all the creatures whose breath, in winter, forms delicate ice crystals in the gaps in the rocks. Still, they would fail to turn over every stone, to unwind every mystery, to unearth every secret. Still, the full expression of the cliff would elude them, passing like water between their fingers.

Beside the cliff, a red oak had embarked on a decades-long adventure, reaching an impossibly long and slender limb over a shelf of bare rock and toward a single beam of precious light. After years of searching it was finally illuminated, so heavy with acorns that it bent like a bow. I listened to the sound of Bear Island Brook, the whirling song of a veery, the distant rush of the highway. Even as we marvel at our power and our genius, we still cannot make an acorn, still cannot say with certainty how or why this year the oak trees were heavy with seed when last year their branches were empty. We still cannot trace the story of every acorn as they are eaten and cached, their energy absorbed by the bodies of the deer and the bears and the chipmunks. We still cannot follow the acorns as a precious few sprout, a tiny fraction reaching above the deer browse, fewer still attaining the canopy, fewer still becoming huge, branching oaks.

The cliff and the oak were just two minuscule pieces of a forest that was itself just a fragment of biosphere that remains largely a mystery. Of the ten million to perhaps thirty million species on earth, only about two million are known to science. Of the known species, many of the nuances of their behaviors and their interactions—how they knit into communities and eco-systems, how they affect our lives and our world—have yet to be discovered.

As I walked along the cliff, even my body was a biological and ecological riddle that defied our understanding. Like every other organism on earth, I was the product of millions of years of adaptation, a link in an evolutionary chain that stretched out of sight. Like the trees in the forest, human bodies are entities and also ecosystems—habitats that harbor their own biodiversity. About 90 percent of the cells in our bodies are bacteria, perhaps ten thousand species of which live on and in us, around six hundred species of which are endemic to our mouths alone. Our skin is like the bark of an ancient tree, home to a rich microbiome of a thousand species of bacteria, fungi, and invertebrates. These organisms form a community of value and purpose and beauty that is integral to our health and well-being, and still we know precious little about it.

I turned away from the cliff, climbing another overgrown skid trail. Clouds painted the sky above, carrying rainwater in their boughs. The clouds were seeded by trees that were members of intricate natural communities, trees that were communities in their own right, trees that were once acorns planted by chattering blue jays, their bodies sustained by insects gleaned from the limbs of countless oaks. The forest on the mountain was a world of unimaginable complexity and nuance; already, I had the humility to know that I could walk along every cliff and up every trail, across every brook, past every tree, and I would still never grasp the entirety of this ecosystem.

The trail carried me into another patch of diseased beech, another dystopian forest. I sighed. We have built our lives on the back of a creature that we do not fully understand: a biosphere of incredible beauty and resilience, a living world of depths that will remain forever undiscovered. The forest on the mountain was alive, its complexity surrounding me, filling me, escaping me. I would never truly know how my actions would ripple throughout this community, the effect that I would have on every being that called this forest home. In this moment, I needed to have the humility to understand this and the courage to act anyway. I would not let uncertainty and fear keep me from doing what was necessary to help this forest reach toward abundance again.

I took another roll of orange flagging out of my vest, wondering what it meant to be the steward of an ecosystem in a world of such shifting and secret dimensions.

I walked the edges of another patch cut, hanging ribbon after orange ribbon. Bear Island spread around me like a broken star. Life hid under every leaf, birds fluttering from branches, trees and plants filling the holes in the world. The abundance of the summer forest masked a delicate and cracked foundation: after millennia of adaptation and change, this forest was forced to hold too many things at once. I could almost feel it straining against the limits of its resilience.

I hung the last piece of orange flagging and turned inward, fighting through the beech brush to the center of the patch cut. Among the diseased beech, I found a few beacons of hope: a red oak, a white pine, a red pine, a red spruce, a service berry. I lifted my paint gun, marking each healthy tree with a bright blue *x*. In a month, these trees would stand alone in field of stumps. In the years ahead, they would be *legacy trees*, elders standing in crowds of children. Across decades, they would witness this forest's regeneration, watch as a living community is reborn from the depths of tragedy. As this forest of the future rises around them, I hoped that they would bear witness to a profound transformation; that their seeds would fall on fertile ground, that their children would spread roots into the deepening soils of a better world.

Painted lady butterflies flitted through the air in front of me, dressed in orange and black and white. I approached a rare healthy beech tree, laying a hand on its smooth gray bark. Perhaps an evolutionary secret was written in the genome of this beech, some genetic gift that made it resistant to beech bark disease. Perhaps its children would also be healthy and strong, with bark as smooth and as silver as the skin of an elephant. Perhaps smooth-barked beech trees would multiply and spread across the mountain, and in some distant century, this would be a forest of healthy beech again. The chance might be one in one million, perhaps far less, but I would take those odds. Even as beech undermined this forest's health, its diversity, its habitat, even as I went to great measures to fight against it, the smooth-barked beech reminded me that beech is one of my favorite tree species. I remembered that my goal is not to eradicate beech—that, more than anything, I wanted to help build a forest of healthy beech again.

I squeezed the paint gun's trigger, marking the beech with a blue *x*.

The feller-buncher sends another bouquet of trees whistling to the ground. I stand in the burning light of a new patch cut, listening to the crashing and the grinding of the machines, marveling at the ease with which the mechanical masters the biological. The feller-butcher's saw is a blur, severing wood layered over decades in a second, changing the forest forever in the blink of an eye.

My body inhales, completing a ritual millions of years in the making. The oxygen that fills my lungs is biological in origin, exhaled by trees and plants as sunlight bathes their tender leaves, as they flower and fruit, as they reach toward the sun. It is a gift given freely by the green life of the biosphere, a vital and invaluable resource produced by ecosystems that ask nothing more than to be allowed to exist.

Below me, the highway hums through the divided floodplain, connecting the fragmented pieces of the broad valley. A train rushes east, blowing its horn. In a world marked by so many monuments to human power, it takes humility to admit that we are dependent on so many things that our incredible technology cannot replace or control. Even as our technology advances and our intelligence grows, even as our cities rise into the sky, even as we infiltrate and alter every natural community on earth, we remain reliant on ecosystems for the air that we breathe, the water that we drink, the food that we eat, the delicate climate that we inhabit. As we search for high-tech solutions to the symptoms of global change, we inhabit a biosphere that is low-tech and elegantly brilliant, already capable of providing so many of the things that we need to survive and to thrive. As far as we have come, we are still tethered to ecosystems—we cannot, and will not, live without them.

The grapple-skidder turns, blowing black smoke into the summer woods. We already have the power to save this living world and to save ourselves in the process. Our challenge is to find the humility to recognize the preciousness of ecosystems and to access the vision to protect them. The future of this forest, of every ecosystem on earth, of our own species, will be written by the choices that we make: the way we manage ecosystems and the way we manage ourselves—the way we change them, the way we change ourselves.

Ten days ago, as the acorns ripened in the oaks, I walked with the loggers, a father and son. The father, Ray, was quiet, peering at the forest through his glasses. Mel and I chatted about work, timber markets, and mutual friends.

The trail crested the first rise, and we stopped in front of a marked patch cut. As the orange flagging fluttered in the wind, I told Ray and Mel that I wanted every tree in the patches cut except for those marked with a blue *x*. They nodded, taking in the stunted red maple, the dying white birch, the diseased beech, the endless beech clones. We all knew that these trees had little, if any, financial value. Though I usually worked with loggers with smaller equipment, I had called Ray and Mel because I knew that only a fully mechanized logging crew could afford to cut so many small and unhealthy trees. Even with their large and efficient equipment, I knew that this job would be commercially marginal at best.

We turned off the main trail and into one of the marked patches, occasionally seeing a larger oak or sugar maple or white pine. Each time, Ray and Mel's faces would lift for a moment and then fall as they saw that each healthy, valuable tree was marked with a blue *x*. I knew that Ray and Mel were struggling to understand why I did not want to harvest every last valuable tree. I knew that they were asking themselves, Why not wring the last drops of value from this forest?

The loggers who high-graded this mountain three decades ago would have agreed. To them, the oaks, the sugar maples, the pines were "mature": of an age or size of maximum economic value. To them, trees were fruits to be plucked. To fail to do so would be to let them rot on the vine.

To me, the oaks, the sugar maples, and the pines were the foundation of the forest of the future, a forest that I hoped would someday be a greater gift to the people and the creatures of this troubled and beautiful world. To me, Ray and Mel's machines were not tools for extracting value, not tools for harvesting a crop, not tools for taking something from this forest. They were tools of cultivation, tools that I would use to plant the seeds of a better world.

I had worked with Ray and Mel before, and I knew that they were honest, trustworthy, and capable. I knew that they would honor their agreements and do what I asked them to do. I also knew that they had earned a reputation for stripping, liquidating, and high-grading forests; that when left to their own devices, they were no different than the last loggers who visited the mountain. Like a chainsaw, they could degrade and destroy this forest. Like a chainsaw, they could also help it heal.

We stopped by another marked patch cut, its understory choked with thousands of finger-sized beech saplings. We stood in silence, Mel shaking his head, Ray polishing his glasses on his stained T-shirt. This job was barely worth their time, but it had been a wet summer, and Ray and Mel had been idling at home, waiting for soils to dry. They were desperate to find any place where their equipment would not be mired in the mud, desperate to get their machines moving, desperate to generate revenue, to keep their employees from looking for work elsewhere, to make equipment payments of tens of thousands of dollars each month.

The afternoon light was gentle, the air warm and sweet on my skin. Nothing was clear, nothing easy, nothing certain. I thought about my plan for this forest, wondering if there was something that I was missing. Anxiety tagged my mind, asking me if I was any different from the people who degraded this forest, if I was doomed to make the same mistakes all over again. I wondered if the foresters of the future would walk this trail and shake their heads at me, just as I shook my head at the foresters and the loggers of the past. I wondered if they would marvel at how little I knew, how wrong I was, if my actions and my choices would seem shortsighted and arrogant in the light of some distant future. I listened to the sounds of the forest, fear begging me to do nothing.

We turned and descended the trail, squirrels chattering at us, the summer sun filtering through the beech leaves. We passed back through the marked patch cuts, the orange flagging flickering from the sides of the trail.

A deer crossed the trail in front of us, shining in her summer coat. In a flash, I remembered my first hunting season, more than a decade ago. I remembered crosshairs tremoring over a doe as she flowed through an autumn forest, remembered the rifle, smooth and hard in my child's hands, its wooden stock pressing coldly against my cheek. I remembered raising the rifle, lowering it, raising and lowering it again. I remembered the sound of my ragged breath as I watched the doe fade into the autumn forest, my mind flooded with shame. It was not until many years later that I learned that I could love deer and kill deer, that I could love trees and kill trees, and that to do so could be an act of profound courage and compassion.

I held this forest in the crosshairs now, my hands trembling. As the acorns hung like brown jewels from the oaks, the biosphere withered around me; its brilliance fading, species everywhere declining and fading out of existence. As birds sang from the canopy, people's lives were swept under the sea, burned to cinders, destroyed by the vagaries of global change. As the forest on the mountain grew and changed, the world was degraded both by people who did too much and by those who did nothing.

I was afraid of failing in my responsibility toward this forest, this forgotten treasure still shining goldenly on the mountain. I was afraid of failing the forests and the people of the world, the bears and the painted ladies, the trees and the mycorrhizal fungi, the children blinking into existence on this August day. I reached for the humility to accept that the choices I made would always be flawed, that I would always take some steps forward and some steps back. I reached for the humility to wade in the waters of uncertainty, to recognize that the duality of right and wrong would never do my choices justice. I was learning that there were no easy answers to fight for, but that we must fight anyway. I was learning that if we wait to be certain, if we demand perfection, we will do nothing at all.

The forest on the mountain leaned over us, bright and hard and stark, blue sky stretched over towering rock. It was a system that thrived on both efficiency and inefficiency—both harmonious and disharmonious, both altruistic and individualistic. The beauty of the forest was carried not in one simple truth but in a trillion unimaginable realities. So many opposite things thrived in the forest without contradiction. So many disparate things were true.

We rounded the last corner, breaking back into the light of the clearing. I wondered if humility was what separated me from the foresters and the loggers of the past, if humility was what made me different from the people who mythologized this forest and from those who treated it as a commodity. I wondered if it was humility, not certainty, that would help me be a true steward of this forest: if it would help me do what was necessary to protect this precious thing, if it would help me have the vision to change.

The machines are gone, their engines roaring over some distant mountain.

The log landing is the surface of an alien planet, barren and empty, shadows leaning ominously. For weeks the landing was a hive of activity, an unending crush of trucks and chippers and skidders. Now it is quiet again, filled only with a ringing, buzzing void. I pull on my orange vest and begin to climb the main skid trail, the smell of turned earth filling my body.

The main trail winds through the first patch cut, an acre of naked oaks and scarred earth. I walk in silence, sweat stinging my eyes, acorns sliding beneath my boots. The more that I work to protect and to care for ecosystems, the more I recognize this feeling: the emptiness that follows a profound compromise.

The trail is chafed and roughened, its orange mineral soil exposed by the metal tracks of the feller-buncher, the chain-wrapped tires of the skidders, the dragging bodies of trees beyond counting. Over the last month, Ray and Mel's machines cut thousands of trees and dragged them to the landing. There, they were sliced into timber, pulp, firewood, and chips, loaded onto trucks, carried away. I had watched the loggers work, feeling both the weight of so many endings and the promise of so many new beginnings.

The wood that the loggers pulled from the mountain would never be deadwood on the forest floor, would never be habitat for spotted salamanders, would never be nourishment for the fungi or the trees of the forest. And yet I know that, somewhere, the wood is becoming something radical and beautiful and life-giving after all: somewhere, it is being transformed into energy, into heat, into shelter, into beautiful things. Somewhere it is helping to nourish people who deserve to have warmth and shelter, to live in a beautiful world, to feel freedom and joy and hope. Somewhere, it is a renewable resource in a world where the extraction and use of nonrenewable resources threatens the vitality of the biosphere, its species and its peoples, its waters and its trees, its salamanders and its fungi.

I cross through another patch cut. What a strange world this is, I think. If I wished, I could live my life without understanding or feeling the true impact of my choices. I could say "not in my backyard" to logging while consuming resources that cause untold harm to ecosystems, to species, to peoples across the world—resources produced in faraway places, with costs to ecosystems and peoples that would shock me. If I wished, I could fight for the *illusion of preservation*: for the comfort of myself and the subjugation of those without the privilege of saying "not in my backyard."

The growing body of research around environmental racism, environmental injustice, and climate injustice illuminates the fact that impoverished communities and communities of color are much more likely feel the negative impacts of human consumption—from pollution to climate change—than the privileged. Even as we advocate for justice and equity in our local communities, we can make choices that tacitly support companies, industries, and practices that fuel systems of inequity and injustice around the world. Even as we protect our children, we can doom the children of others to be displaced and oppressed, their lives colonized by our choices.

Below the cliffs, thick black conduit catches the light, sagging through the power line corridor. The wires hum with pure energy, channeling the elemental forces of wind, sunlight, water, and ancient carbon to the people of the valley: lighting their homes and their businesses, warming them and cooling them, illuminating their blinking screens.

It is humbling to recognize that our lives will always come at a cost: that we will always need energy, will always need food and shelter. We will always consume to survive, and our consumption will always impact this biosphere and each other. We cannot choose *if* we want to impact ecosystems, *if* we want to impact peoples across the globe, *if* we want to impact the lives of future generations. Our only choice is, *What do we want our impact to be?* We will make these choices with our eyes open, or we will make them with our eyes closed.

Dust spins through the air, catching the ochre light. I stop to pick up a perfect round acorn, nestling it into the orange soil. I can hear them now: the people who will call these patch cuts a travesty, the people who cannot imagine that the cutting of a tree could be anything other than an expression of domination and colonization, a thoughtless and unhinged use of power. I under-stand their feelings—I hear the same voice inside myself, among a chorus of others. When every instinct told me to embrace a con-venient and comfortable illusion, to pretend that it was enough to do nothing, I walked a different path. I did this not because it was my right; I did this because it was my responsibility.

Once, I envisioned a better world as a landscape of bound-less ecosystems, unaffected by people. Now, I see a better world as one where humans are actors, not bystanders, where we are brave and humble and imbued with responsibility. It is a world in which beauty may be found in both a managed forest and an unmanaged forest, in a fresh stump and in a tree that will never be timber. It is a world in which we understand that all of these things must exist for any of them to exist, in which we recognize that all of these things are complementary and compatible and essential.

In a time when the impacts of our lives are so often shipped away to some distant forest, some distant people, there is something profound about taking ownership of this moment: the discomfort and the sadness and the upheaval and the compromise that is the cost of a human life embodied. I have been offered a thousand easier paths, but I have chosen to bring this feeling home, to carry a piece of it inside of me, and it feels radical.

Across a smoldering patch cut, I can see Honey Hollow creasing the western mountains, the secret valley of Gleason Brook, the high crest of the sitting-place mountain. I watch the cars on the highway, the thin line of the train tracks, listen to the buzz of a helicopter overhead. I am reminded why I call this place an island: I stand on the edge of tens of thousands of acres of forest, the currents of the human world rushing around me.

An ancient yellow birch is a bronze statue in the patch's center, the shattered stumps of beech saplings like corn stubble at its feet. Through so much death, I know that Bear Island is at the beginning of a profound transformation, that it is in the process of becoming something new.

Through the scorching silence, I hear the words of the poet William Stafford: "Your job is to find out what the world is trying to be." I believe that this forest is trying to be vibrant and healthy, alive and changing, resilient and abundant. I believe that it is trying to be a small piece of a better world—a world that is a massive, composite being, a world that is both this biosphere and its people, a world that is something complex and imperfect, emergent and greater than the sum of its parts. I believe that this forest cannot be planned and regulated, that it cannot live in captivity. I believe that this world must create itself, and I believe it will not become what it is trying to be on its own.

I watch clouds drift over Honey Hollow and dream of this forest as it may someday be, when my time as its steward draws to a close. Decades from now, I will walk through this patch cut, my hands worn and calloused, my face creased by watersheds of smile lines. I will rest my hand on the shining trunk of a young oak and remember, distantly, the emptiness of this moment. I hope that I will have lived a life of joy and kindness and meaning. I hope that I will have been brave enough to act and humble enough to change. I hope that along my stuttering path, I will have always tried to do better, to be better. I hope that I will have worked hard to understand this forest and my role in it more fully, while letting it remain an exquisite mystery.

Dusk rolls over the mountain. I untether my mind and let it drift through dreams of hope. Today, within this massive, incomprehensible, interconnected reality, my dream seems out of reach and also, somehow, possible. I ask for the courage to change this place and for the humility to let it be itself, in all its beauty.

9 RESILIENCE: OF BUMBLEBEES AND BARBERRY

I pull the trigger. The thin blue mist catches the light, whispering onto the Japanese barberry's leaves. Sweat runs down my temples, soaking my shirt, filling my rubber gloves. The barberry bushes fill the forest's understory like a choking smog.

The September sun shines through an exhausted forest. In May, the birds arrived here in their colors, sang their songs and made their extravagant displays, guarded clutches of speckled eggs. The trees of the forest expanded from every edge, gilding themselves with perfect new leaves. Summer came and the waiting world was filled with life.

Today, the eggs have hatched, the chicks fledged, the birds gone south again. The trees and the plants have grown, flowered, and set seed, and now they wait for winter, next spring's buds hardening on their twigs. Everything has happened, and now the forest settles into the buzzing rhythm of September: the goldenrod time, the aster time, a time that is both an ending and a beginning.

I pause, adjusting the straps of the backpack sprayer on my aching shoulders. I have walked this mountain all summer with this tank on my back, searching for barberry, for honeysuckle, for glossy buckthorn, for bittersweet vines and the arching canes of multiflora rose. My eyes have become as attuned to them as a lynx is to the flick of a snowshoe hare's ear, as a trout is to an insect landing on the shimmering surface of the water. I see them when I blink, and in the shifting landscapes of my dreams.

The tank sloshes as I scramble upward. Ahead of me, my shadow looms; the profile of a bulging insect, tilting and lumbering up the shins of the mountain. I remember the day that I first saw this place; when I followed a queen bumblebee across this slope, hoping to find a garden of *Dicentra*. I remember my shirt, cold on my chest, as I paused, looked once and looked again. I remember the moment when I realized that it was Japanese barberry that spread across the folds of the hillside, filling its ravines and creeping up its brown ridges. I had never seen an infestation so dense and so expansive. It seemed to fill the world, vibrating with an alien frequency.

I steady myself, plant my feet, and begin to spray again. On that day, one year ago, I thought that there was no future for this forest, no hope. A year later, this forest has become my responsibility. I want to live in a better world, and so I pull the trigger again, spraying herbicide into the heat of a waning Vermont summer.

My right hand swings the lever up and down in an uneven rhythm. My left pulls the trigger, guiding the wand over the barberry's whorled leaves. I encircle the bush, color its leaves with herbicide, move to the next. The wand flies from plant to plant, faster and faster. I pump and spray, pump and spray, my mind singing Iggy and the Stooges: "Search and Destroy." Soon I am on fire, sweeping the understory with blue flames, drums pounding, guitars snarling in my mind. I trip, stumble, catch myself and pause, breathing deeply. A raven croaks from a pine tree overhead. A cool breeze touches my face.

The living things that make up this forest community are ancient. Over millennia they have formed and filled unique niches, have found their way in this world and with one another. Over unfathomable expanses of time, the earth has given rise to millions of species, each unique, each touching ecosystems and each other in different ways. *Biodiversity*—the variation between ecosystems, species, and the genetics within each individual species—has bloomed throughout the biosphere, life filling every crevice of this abundant planet.

Today, this biodiversity is at risk. An estimated one million animal and plant species are threatened with extinction, including more than 40 percent of amphibians, one-third of reef-forming corals, and more than one-third of marine mammals. At least 680 vertebrate species and 100,000 species of invertebrates have gone extinct since the sixteenth century, and, according to the World Wildlife Fund, global animal populations have declined an average of 68 percent since 1970.

I listen to my heartbeat slow, watching the late summer light wander through the leaves. Tens of thousands of species make their lives in this forest. They are predators and prey, animals as massive as a moose and as small as a nematode. There are white pines that may grow 150 feet tall and service berries that may only grow fifteen feet tall, oaks whose lives may span six centuries and insects that live only hours or days. There are plants that bloom in spring, summer, and fall, those that live in the shade and those that live in the open. There are maidenhair ferns growing in rich hollows and bracken ferns on the sandy flats. There are birds fluttering through the trees and millipedes tunneling through the duff. There are so many shapes of life in this forest, so many ways of being, so many irreplaceable things.

Every time I walk this hillside, I see two realities: the world that is here and the world that is missing. In May this slope should be covered in *ephemerals*—the enigmatic spring wildflowers that bloom in the brief window between when the soil thaws and when the leaves of the trees unfurl. Once, centuries ago, I am certain that the understory of this forest was a garden of ephemerals—*Dicentra* and wild ginger, purple *Hepatica*, tiny spring beauties, toothworts, bloodroot and blue cohosh, red and white and painted trilliums. Now it is only barberry.

I listen to the chattering woods, to the crickets' drone that marks the beginning of the end of summer. Soon it will be autumn, then winter. In April, the sun will warm the earth again, and I will wander through Vermont's naked forests, the leaves of the trees still sleeping in their buds, listening to the brown creeper's tinkling song, searching for a splash of green. When I finally find it, I will stretch my body over the fragrant duff to stare a fuzzy *Hepatica* straight in the eye, to admire the gothic architecture of an unfurling blue cohosh, to expose the strange, rigid flower of wild ginger, blooming beneath the matted leaves. It is impossible to say if I love the ephemerals so much because of their singular beauty, because they are strange and fleeting, or because they are a symbol of the forest's awakening—the first plants to grow after a long winter. All that I know is that they are precious to me.

I am not the only one in this forest that loves ephemerals. For thousands of years the *Dicentra* sisters—"squirrel corn" and "Dutchman's breeches"—have opened their flowers on this hillside just as queen bumblebees, *Dicentra's* nearly sole pollinator, emerged from the earth. For thousands of years, the spring beauty miner bee flew through the understory of this forest, visiting only the painted petals of the spring beauties. For thousands of years, the fetid odor of wild ginger and red trillium (also known as "wake robin" or "stinking Benjamin") attracted gnats, beetles, and flies as they foraged for carrion in the thawing forest. For thousands of years, lines of ants carried the seeds of bloodroot, *Dicentra*, and trillium across the mountain, planting gardens of ephemerals.

The symbioses between these insects and the ephemerals are often considered mutualisms: relationships from which each species benefits. They are beautiful and bittersweet things. While mutualisms are important to the function and the resilience of ecosystems, in this world of extinction and invasion and fragmentation they may also be a source of vulnerability— I wonder where the spring beauty miner bees go when there are no spring beauties, where the queen bumblebee goes to break her winterlong fast when there are no Dutchman's breeches on the mountain. Today the ephemerals are exiles, lost to this place. I wonder what else is missing.

The native species that compose this forest are vital and irreplaceable, the living threads that stitch this community together. The insects and the ephemerals, the fungi of the soil, the creatures of the rhizosphere and the necrosphere, the birds and the bats—these things are not simply a byproduct of a healthy forest. They are fingers on the same hand, branches on the same tree, as integral to the health and the function of this forest as an organ is to my body. As I reimagine this forest and what it means to care for it, I know that I cannot love and protect it without loving and protecting all the native species that call it home.

I pump the lever, feeling the pressure in the tank tighten, my mind soft again. In this world of fallen things, it is too easy to get lost in the negative. I pull the trigger, coating another barberry bush in herbicide. I remind myself that this is an act of genera-tion—not destruction—that I am here to manifest life, not death. I kill the barberries not because I hate them but because I love this forest so deeply. I think of the ephemerals and remember that I am not here to destroy an enemy. I am here to help a friend.

As I walk across the mountain, I feel less like I am searching and destroying and more like I am freeing some giant, tender animal, unwinding the strangling threads that bind it. One day I hope to see it roam free again.

I move across the hill, the sweet, acrid smell of herbicide follow-ing me. Though they do not yet know it, the barberries behind me are already dead. The herbicide will find its way into their vessels, their yellow roots, to the tip of each thorny finger. In a few weeks their leaves will shrivel like wet paper. In a few more this will be a boneyard, their skeletons stained faintly blue.

Japanese barberry was brought to North America as an ornamental plant, a decoration for yards and gardens. It escaped, spreading through the half-light of the forest edges and into the woods, its seeds carried far and wide by birds and bears and rodents. Released from the competitors, parasites, pathogens, and environmental contrasts of its native ecosystems, the bar-berry was hypercompetitive, able to grow nearly anywhere, and nearly impossible to kill—a suite of traits common to nearly all invasive plants.

Barberry is just one of many species that have been introduced into this valley and the valleys beyond over the last several centuries. The seas and the skies of the earth have become porous; humans have both intentionally and unintentionally facilitated a migration of plants, animals, pests, and pathogens at a scope, scale, and speed unprecedented in the history of this planet. Of the nonnative species that are introduced into new environments, the vast majority are benign. Only a small portion are *invasive*—outcompeting native species and causing substantial harm to ecosystems—but these few are disruptive enough to threaten the function, integrity, and resilience of ecosystems and biodiversity across the globe. According to the National Wildlife Federation, 42 percent of endangered species are primarily threatened by invasive plants, animals, pests, and pathogens, and invasives account for about half of the extinctions of which the cause is known. Globally, the major threats to biodiversity are often abbreviated by the acronym HIPPO: Habitat loss, Invasive species, human Population, Pollution, and Overharvesting.

As I spray, Bear Island leans over me, singular and imperfect. Like every ecosystem, the forest on the mountain is defined by what it *is*—the oak and the beech, the bear and the deer, the bumblebees and the *Dicentra*—and also by what it is *not*—the niches that were never filled, the species that are not here, the evolutionary doors that have remained unopened. In their shared journey across unthinkable spans of time, the native species of this forest have adapted only to each other, coevolving with just a tiny fraction of the earth's flora and fauna. Over millennia of life and death, relationship and competition, parasitism and predation, they have formed elaborate physical, chemical, and behavioral traits that have allowed them to coexist in a dynamic equilibrium with one another.

This isolation of ecosystems from one another across their evolutionary histories has made ecosystems unique and diverse and also vulnerable. The trees of this forest suffer from beech bark disease, chestnut blight, butternut canker, and Dutch elm disease—an array of nonnative pathogens that are benign in their native environments, normal and natural parts of some faraway forest. In this forest they are deadly, powerful enough to change the behavior of these tree species, and the biological communities that surround them, forever. Five miles west of Bear Island, the emerald ash borer expands its reach; soon the white ash trees of the mountain, the green ash of the valley bottoms, and the black ash of the swamps will all be gone. An endless parade of other invasive plants, pests, and pathogens knock at the door of this forest, threatening to undermine the pieces of it that remain.

The lobed leaves of a red oak seedling spread defiantly through the barberry. I move the little oak aside with my foot, spray the barberry, and release it. Across oceans, I know that red oak, black cherry, the American mink, and the American bullfrog—species that are all integral parts of this forest community—are invasive, undermining the function and the integrity of ecosystems and causing billions of dollars of damage to them. It is odd to think that red oak, a species that carries so much of my hope for this forest, could ever be a biodiversity threat. At the same time, I know that in some distant ecosystem barberry is a member of a unique biological community with its own ancient and enigmatic relationships, an ecosystem threatened by its own suite of invasives.

I spray another barberry bush. The forest around me is not entirely bereft of life; above my head, the wind tousles the leaves of the trees. In June, birds hid their nests in the barberry's arching stems, and I watched them flick their tail feathers, hopping from limb to thorny limb. I have seen bobcats stalking through the multiflora rose thickets along the highway, have seen cedar waxwings foraging in the buckthorn berries, have seen bees visiting the honeysuckle flowers.

While some of Bear Island's native species may use the invasive plants, the barberry will never foster the complex web of connections and relationships known to the many native species that it outcompetes. As chickadees forage on the honeysuckle, they will find only a tiny fraction of the invertebrates that live on native plants. As songbirds feed on buckthorn berries, they will find that these berries lack the nourishment that they need to make their incredible seasonal migrations. As invasive plants spread their roots downward, they will alter the chemical and microbial composition of the soil, even inhibiting the mycorrhizal fungi that native trees and plants rely on. As the invasives dominate the forest's understory, they will outcompete the native trees and plants, derailing the natural processes—growth, death, regeneration—that make this ecosystem function, that make it glow and flourish, that give it the power to heal and to change.

The barberry is a champion of the Anthropocene, a hero of this bleeding world, this changing climate, this fragmented landscape, these altered and threatened ecosystems. In a world in which only some earn the right to survive, it thrives. As it does, many others may be lost.

I follow a trail of barberry bushes onto a broad, flat bench. Above me, a wolf tree reaches its branches outward, framed against the shining cliffs. The wolf tree is a white ash, a species that my future children may know only as snags leaning overhead, as scores of naked trunks littering the forest floor, as another mythic creature lost to this modern world.

The bench is bright with barberry stems, their thorns soft and green, a meadow of root sprouts. Two months ago, I spent a long day hand-pulling barberry at the feet of the wolf tree, chasing their roots with my hands and my shovel as they twisted and dove through the flinty soil. After eight hours I stumbled to my feet, sweaty and dehydrated, my fingernails broken, thorns embedded in my fingers, my back and my shoulders stiff. The bench was littered with upturned barberry bushes, no more than a tenth-acre of thorny stems and broken soil. As the light dimmed, I leaned on the patterned bark of the wolf tree and looked over my work. I knew that in truth I had done nothing, that countless yellow root fragments still lingered in the soil, each destined to resprout. Down the hill, twenty acres of barberry spread in every direction, impenetrable and impossible.

The sunlight passed though the wolf tree's tattered canopy, dappling the forest floor. For thousands of years this forest had regenerated and changed, had made and remade itself in countless iterations. For thousands of years, this forest was healthy not because it was stable but because it was resilient: a living system so dynamic, so adapted to stress and to hardship, that it could not be broken. I knew that soon the wolf tree, and the other ash trees on the mountain, would die. As it always had, the forest would reach for the miracle of regeneration, for its incredible ability to find diversity in adversity, to chase death with life. This time, it would not come. As trees died, as gaps opened in the forest canopy, the barberry would spread, thicken, fill every space. The barberry would tighten its grip on the understory, holding the future of this forest hostage.

As the climate changed in dramatic and unpredictable ways, as seasons shifted, as new pests and pathogens emerged, as native species were lost and new species were introduced, I knew that this forest needed to do more than just recover. It needed to adapt, to reinvent itself in profound ways. This forest and its biological community stood at a threshold, its resilience more needed and more under threat than ever before. It could not move forward alone.

I watched the ocean of barberry, holding my throbbing hands against my chest. I felt as helpless and powerless and small as I had in the months after my eye injury, a decade before. I was lost and alone, standing on the banks of another river that I could not cross. Ten years before, as my world lay in ruins around me, I was faced with a choice. I could deflect and deny, could pretend that my life could be just as it was before my accident. Or I could find the courage and the humility to face my trauma and to move forward, even if that meant becoming something else.

As my one working eye swept across the acres of barberry, I knew that no amount of tenacity and willpower would make hand-pulling the barberry enough. I knew that if I wanted to truly heal this forest, I would need to accept that it was not enough to try, not enough to make a gesture of compassion. I needed to accept the truth of my situation and the bitter reality of what would be necessary to solve this problem. As scary and as uncomfortable as it felt, I needed to adapt.

Ten years ago, lost in trauma, I could not have imagined that I had arrived at a beginning as much as an ending. I could not have imagined that I would trace everything good in my life back to my accident and the months that followed. Today, I have learned my true capacity for resilience. Today, I have learned that it is my scars that make me strong and brave and beautiful. Today, I see my accident as a moment that incited a process of regeneration, a doorway that opened toward the person I am proud to have become.

Ten years ago, when my life lay in pieces around me, I found hope in the abundance of life: in the beaked hazelnut flowers and the spring ephemerals, in the trees and the bees and the butterflies of the forest. I found purpose in the practice of forestry, in the crooked beauty of searching for a way for people and ecosystems to exist together. In time, I learned to be like a forest: to bloom through my wounds, to regenerate through the rubble, to move toward the future with hope. I learned that if I allowed myself to change, there were no boundaries to what I might become.

Ten years ago, I could not have imagined how relationship and responsibility would change me. I could not have imagined that someday I would spray herbicide into a forest that I love, and that this would be a radical expression of humility and love. On this September day, I have become something radical and emergent. I have adapted, my resilience carrying me to strange and beautiful places. Like me, this forest is a cracked vessel. Like me, it is a process, never completed. Neither this forest nor I will ever be perfect, but I am proud of what we are becoming together.

I pull the trigger again. As many times as I repeat this action, as familiar as it has become, it still feels surreal. This herbicide was created to suppress biodiversity, to kill weeds in endless monocultures of corn and wheat and soybeans. Across the world, it is used in ways that threaten the health of people and wildlife and ecosystems, in ways that pollute our soils and our food and our waters. All of this is true.

And this is also true: in my hands, the herbicide is a tool used to *protect* biodiversity—to safeguard the integrity of this ecosystem and the lives of its inhabitants, to help an alien monoculture become a vibrant community again. I have turned this chemical toward resilience and abundance, an act as subversive and oddly beautiful as a chainsaw thrumming in my hands.

My right hand swings the pump, my left directing the wand. I remember the first day that I sprayed herbicide at Bear Island: how the backpack sprayer felt unfamiliar on my shoulders, how dissonance crowded my mind each time that I pulled the trigger. At the end of that day, as the sun sank toward the Adirondacks, acres of barberry leaves glowed sapphire and green. Somehow, my heart swelled with joy. I felt that I had done something profound and brave, something truly and deeply important. In a forest where I once felt only hopelessness, it seemed that the tides were finally turning toward life.

Some will say that using herbicide makes me careless, thoughtless, negligent. Others will say that I am wasting my time. Perhaps they are right, but I think not. I am doing what I must to protect this forest and the creatures and the people whose lives depend on it, reaching toward abundance and resilience with my eyes wide open. I am doing what I can with the power and the freedom that I have, taking up the mantle of responsibility that awaits us all, should we choose to accept it.

Once, I thought that being radical meant forming views as hard, as uncompromising, as unchanging as stone. Now, I believe that what is truly radical is to be as dynamic as a forest: to have the courage to adapt, to change, to constantly reimagine my relationship with this ecosystem and this glowing world. I have learned that the steps on the path toward a better world are often counterintuitive, uncomfortable, and strange. I have learned that what is simple is rarely true and what is necessary is rarely easy.

The highway drones in my ears, the unending soundtrack to Bear Island's lower world. Barberry and buckthorn and honeysuckle bushes huddle between its rushing lanes, crowding its shoulders, their limbs heavy with fruit.

I turn north, tracing the fragments of barbed wire that mark Bear Island's western boundary. On my neighbor's land, the barberry bushes spread out of sight, their red berries winking at me. Like me, my neighbor has the privilege of being a landowner, the steward of a piece of the forest on the mountain. Like me, he is afforded broad freedoms within our connected reality. I use my freedom to control the invasives that threaten the future of this ecosystem. My neighbor uses his freedom to ignore them.

In the coming years, I will find that the barberries from my neighbor's land have sent their seeds across this boundary, that the invasives in the powerline corridor and on the shoulders of the highway have manifested insurgent populations of barberry and bittersweet, buckthorn and garlic mustard, multiflora rose and honeysuckle at Bear Island. Each year, I will return with my backpack sprayer, each year spraying a little less, each year dreaming of the year when I will not spray at all. It may never come. As I walk this slope in the heat of endless summers, I will resist frustration and despair, reaching for the resilience needed to undertake a task that is brutal and vital and never ending.

In this strange world, I am an outlier and my neighbor's inaction is normal. Most people are completely unaware of invasive species and the threats that they pose to the ecosystems that make life on this planet possible. Some, like my neighbor, are aware of the invasives but scoff at the idea that they might have some responsibility to control them.

Like climate change, invasives and the measures necessary to control them are inconvenient truths. Faced with the prospect of such massive inconveniences and compromises, many people view invasives through the lens of *confirmation bias*—ignoring the consensus of wildlife biologists, ecologists, foresters, and the scientific community, developing elaborate philosophies that justify the presence of the invasives and our inaction toward them. Some say that ecosystems will simply adapt to invasives, as if the evolutionary history of this forest will be rewritten overnight. Some say that invasives are the biosphere's answer to global change, that they are in some way here to save us. Part of me wishes that I could be swept away by such comforting illusions, that I could tell myself a story that would free me from my responsibility. As much as I would love to live a fantasy, I will not. I will have the humility to accept the bitter truth, as inconvenient and as uncomfortable as it may be.

I reach the cliffs and turn down the hill again. This summer, I have spent every weekend spraying plant-killing chemicals into a forest that I love. Day after day, I have filled my tank, measuring out the herbicide, surfactant, water, and dye. Day after day, I have trudged through waist-high barberry, swinging the wand over its bright and hopeful leaves. Each time that I question myself, I look up at the cliffs and remember that, once, the rocks of this mountain were empty. I remember the miracle of biodiversity: that, over eons, life found its way here in so many strange and beautiful ways, a barren world becoming home to so many irreplaceable things.

I often wonder how many pieces we could remove from a forest, how many timbers we could pull from this wooden tower before it finally collapses. The truth is that this forest is already collapsing, already off the edges of every map, already beyond the limits of its resilience. Even without the invasive plants, animals, pests, and pathogens, even without a mass extinction, even without the legacies of clearing and mismanagement, even without deer overpopulations, the effects of climate change alone would be enough to threaten the integrity and the function of this forest. Today, the forest on the mountain must face all these things at once. To ask it to weather this storm without my help would be an act of negligence: toward this ecosystem and its inhabitants, toward the countless people whose lives this forest touches and enriches and supports in some small way, to the future generations who will need healthy forests more than ever.

I cross the mountain, the smell of the herbicide heavy in the air. From somewhere deep in the talus of my mind I remember that this forest is built of lives beyond counting, of pieces and parts that now seem to slide away from it like silk, slipping through its ancient, green fingers. This forest does not care about my fantasies, my philosophies, the stories that I tell myself. It is not comforted or sustained by people who watch it teeter and sink into dysfunction, claiming that inaction is an expression of compassion.

I wish that things could have been different. And yet I know that it does not matter how this forest, or I, arrived at this place. It does not matter how many different turns we could have taken, how many ways things could or should have been. All that matters is what we do now, how we pick up the pieces of this world and try to rebuild something worth saving.

My tank is empty. I turn up the hill toward the clearing, tracing the narrow deer trail that I walked the first time that I visited this land, when I thought that the forest on the mountain was lost forever. I crest the cliffs and walk through a stand of young oaks, their crowns full and open, the bodies of diseased beech trees tangled at their feet. I cross a three-year-old patch cut, now an ocean of green life. I smile, remembering that each little oak in the patch cut was once an acorn in my hand, planted into the orange soil.

As imperfect as they are, I know that my actions mean something to this forest and to the creatures that live here. I am doing what I can in this one forest, in this one short life, in this one precious world. So much has been lost, and so much remains. There is so much life and hope to be discovered.

Winter has passed, and the red maple buds are swelling. Soon the trees of the forest will awaken into another summer, but this is the time of ephemeral things.

I descend the deer trail, passing into the shadows of the lower world. Beneath the cliffs, the barberries are white cages, bleached and brittle. A tiny pool of green catches my eye. A single *Dicentra* is blooming, three white flowers dangling above a whorl of ornate leaves. Somewhere, a queen bumblebee is emerging from the earth, dusting herself off, flying purposefully across the slope. In a forest that was once empty to her, she will find this treasure, will dangle from these white flowers, will inhabit a mutualism that bumblebees and *Dicentra* have built for millennia. In a month, the *Dicentra* will bear seeds, and lines of ants will carry them across the mountain. Someday, this may be a garden of *Dicentra* again.

I wonder how many relationships like this will be rediscovered in a forest without barberry, how many living things will find refuge in this forest as the climate changes, as their habitats are invaded and lost. In the years to come, I imagine the resilience of the forest returning from exile, like a queen bumblebee emerging into the light of another spring. This forest will have a chance to remember diversity and complexity, to regenerate and adapt, to discover how to thrive in this changed and changing world.

This is just the beginning. In the future, this forest will breach endless waves of adversity and upheaval, will face new stressors and threats, will confront novel challenges that strike to the heart of this ancient community. Again and again, I will give myself to this forest. Again and again, I will weather failures, will reimagine myself and my relationship to this place, will make impossible sacrifices. I will change, I will adapt, I will persist. This forest will not stand alone.

Our relationship with this biosphere always has been, and will always be, imperfect. In this moment, it is time for us to step into our role as caretakers—to help ecosystems respond to the legacies of the past, to survive the oppression of the present, and to adapt to the changes of the future. As we trace the sinuous path from invasive species to keystone species, it is time for us to take responsibility for the world that we have created and to make the sacrifices necessary to protect what is precious.

I cross the power line corridor, tracing the highway fence. The resilience of the forest flickers, flashes of green painting the hillside. I brush aside the lifeless arms of a barberry, kneeling to touch a bloodroot, its tiny body piercing the spring air like a scepter.

Time will pass on the mountain and the world will change, bringing inevitable challenges. When they come, the question is if we will resist or adapt, if we will let ourselves be destroyed, or if we will find the resilience and the humility to meet this dynamic world where and how it is. I hope to be as brave as the *Dicentra*, blooming in the hope that someday the world will join me and we will build something of great beauty, piece by shuddering piece.

10 | BEAUTY: TO PLANT AN ACORN

My hands are hard, my forearms coated with dust. In the harsh light of the clearing, there is always more to be done. There are trees to be planted, mulched, pruned, fenced, and mowed around; sticks and stones to be picked; firewood to be bucked and split. I toss another stone on the wheelbarrow and raise its worn handles, heading to the tree line again. On these long summer days, I lose myself in this homestead world, this built world, the world of the orchard and the pasture and the pond, this forest with every limb trained and pruned, this tame creature of my own imagining.

The clearing is shaped like an hourglass, tipping southward. As the years pass, the clearing will mark my time on this land, a place where my dreams and the sweat of my body will be open to the watching world. Today it is still empty, a desert of stumps and shattered wood. I tilt the stones over the bank and turn the wheelbarrow back into the clearing again. I have known this land for just months but already it is precious to me, the place where my heart sits when my vision darkens. Already it feels as if we belong to one another.

My mind does not yet have the colors to imagine what this clearing may someday become. As the wheelbarrow bumps over stumps and ruts, I dare myself to dream that indigo buntings are singing from the oaks, that monarch butterflies are sipping from Joe-pye weed flowers as tall as August corn, that apples are hanging from the trees in the orchard like red moons. The clearing may someday tell a story of a healing that has layered like soil over bedrock, each year more bountiful than the last. It may someday tell a story of relationship and responsibility, freedom and power, beauty and change. Today, these waters still ebb on distant shores. I pick up another stone and lay it on the gathering pile.

The sun sheds a cloud and my eyes are drawn southward, toward the sitting-place mountain. My vision wanders the rough edges of the clearing, the forest leaning over me like a big brother. Above, a raven is quacking from the dead-topped pine and the aspen leaves are shimmering like running water. I stand and rest my hands on my hips. The land I call Bear Island rises toward the cliffs of Stimson Mountain, as unselfconsciously as a black bear running uphill. My eyes chase its contours.

Suddenly, I ache to walk through wild, unvarnished worlds, where history is written in the living soil and in the warm bodies of animals, hunting in the shade. I ache to walk among trees and flowers that will grow in no gardens. I wipe my brow and head south, leaving the human world behind.

The skid trail threads through the patch cuts, these new wounds cleaved in this forest's body, but not its heart. It is an acorn year, and the mountain is alive with the gathering. The crowns of the red oaks bend, weighted with plump seed, acorn caps hanging from their branches like bells. Squirrels crash through the trees as bears probe the ground with their prehensile lips, flocks of turkeys scraping the leathery duff as deer paw and dance around, chewing conspicuously. The leaves are turning: the maples in red and orange, birches in yellow, ash in a muted purple. The forest is dry and dusty, exhausted and ready to sleep, but for the moment everything is rich.

One day I will walk this trail when things seem hopeless and find that the leaves of summer have turned it into a supple jungle. Blackberry canes will loop through sheaves of goldenrod, young birch and oak and aspen reaching hopefully upward, ferns and wildflowers huddled at their feet. Bees and flies will buzz through the air, dodging the spiderwebs that bridge the waving stalks of boneset and snakeroot. Songbirds will hunt and sing, negotiate and bicker with rivals, flit from blackberry to oak with a great sense of importance. Everything will be a glowing mess—brutal and vital, small and massive, simple and complex, making and remaking itself in every instant—and I will remember that a forest wears its scars with pride, sewing up its wounds with golden thread. As the forest hums like a warm machine around me, I will realize that beauty has found its way to this place and find solace in knowing that I helped make it so.

Today, the patch cuts are as naked and as tender as the pink flesh under my fingernails, as empty as tombs. I walk the skid trail, watching the sunlight sink into Bear Island's secret hollows, fighting the urge to wander off. In the years to come, I will walk this trail countless times. I will often start walking with some goal in mind: I will be searching for rogue barberries, tracking deer, seeing if the beaked hazelnuts are blooming at the Four Corners, visiting the cutleaf toothwort along Berta Brook. But, as I enter the sounds and the smells and the shadows of the forest, I will be distracted by the least things. Soon I will be drifting like plankton, carried by the wind toward anything at all.

I feel my acorn-planting stick, rough and perfect in my left hand, and I remember myself. The acorn-planting stick is a narrow stem of hop hornbeam, five feet long, an inch and a half in diameter. Once, the hop hornbeam was a small seed hidden inside a papery packet. Once, it unfurled on the edge of a log landing, becoming a slender tree with tan, peeling bark and wood like iron. Two weeks ago, I cut the hop hornbeam tree with my chainsaw and sharpened one end with my axe. Just as I killed countless trees in the patch cuts so that this forest might be healthy again, I killed the hop hornbeam so that many others could live.

My journey is sinuous, life traded for life. I feel like I am always going down to go up, choosing less to choose more.

I crest the hill. A patch cut spreads across a little valley in front of me, a single oak at its center. I turn to the north and continue upward, acorns sliding under my boots. This year, the acorns are everywhere: falling into streams, wedging into cracks in the rocks, piling thanklessly on suburban lawns. Acorn years like this are *episodic*—occurring only every two to three years—and *synchronous*—after years of few, if any, acorns, this autumn the red oaks across this region are all producing huge crops of seed at once.

Among other potential purposes, *synchrony* is thought to be a form of *predator satiation*, a way that the oaks manipulate the many creatures that eat acorns. The populations of these animals, especially rodents like squirrels and voles, are strongly tied to acorn production—they will skyrocket in the aftermath of an acorn year like this. If acorns were abundant on the mountain every year, the populations of these species would remain high, and all the acorns would be eaten. Instead, for the last two years red oaks across this region have withheld their acorns, starving the squirrels and the mice, lowering their populations through attrition. Now, when their pockets are empty, the oaks overwhelm the creatures of the forest with an unconquerable abundance.

I lean on my acorn-planting stick and consider the genius of synchrony, another chord of brilliance struck by this living world. While theories abound, it is a comfort to me that we still do not know how synchrony occurs—how the oaks know when it is time to flower and to set fruit, and how they tell each other. In this world of answers, we only know that it happens, and that it is vital and beautiful.

The Big Patch is shaped like a heart, curled around a long, low ridge. As I enter it, I remember when I walked this land for the first time, just three months ago. I remember pausing on that ridge, leaning on the bark of a bigtooth aspen and looking down through a forest that was a disconsolate stranger, broken and hopeless. Today, the Big Patch is as open as a savanna. Oaks tilt like palms on a desert island, casting little pools of milky shade. Acorns roll over the bare earth at their feet like unguarded treasure.

I bend and pick up an acorn. It is a good one, unblemished, a rich chocolate brown. On one end is its belly button, the halo where a patterned cap once connected it to its mother tree. On the other, a tiny prickle presses delicately into my fingertip, concealing the acorn's embryo. I thrust my acorn-planting stick into the earth, drop the acorn into the shallow hole, and cover it with soil—planting it with the flat of my palm.

The acorns' abundance masks their vulnerability. Over the two years that it has taken the oaks to grow these acorns, 50–90 percent have been parasitized by acorn weevils and lost to a variety of other pests, parasites, and environmental stressors. Of the acorns that have been lucky enough to reach maturity, 90 percent or more will be eaten or parasitized before ever getting the chance to sprout.

My acorn-planting stick thunks into the baked ground, raising clouds of dust. I plant acorn after acorn, mimicking the practice of *synzoochory*: the way that the squirrels and the voles gather and cache acorns in preparation for winter. In an acorn year, it is common for all acorns left on the surface of the soil to be consumed or destroyed—for the only survivors to be those that have been buried or cached. The relationship between rodents and oaks is another mutualism: the rodents receive the nourishment of the acorns and the oaks receive the benefits of dispersal in return.

Like the relationship between people and ecosystems, the relationship between oaks and rodents is imperfect, and different individuals inhabit it differently. A species is not a monolith: within many wildlife species, the conduct of each individual animal is variable, expressed across a spectrum of behaviors, traits, and tendencies known collectively as *animal personality*. The fate of an acorn depends not just on whether a squirrel or a vole picks it up, but on which individual squirrel or vole it is. Some individuals are more *antagonistic*—more likely to destroy acorns or to cache them in places where they will not sprout—while others are more *mutualistic*, caching viable acorns in ways and in places where they have a chance to someday become oaks. Individual rodents of the latter group, the mutualists, are so important to oak reproduction that some call them *keystone individuals*.

While it was once thought that the rodents, especially squirrels, often forget the location of their caches, we now know that squirrels have excellent spatial memory and that the vast majority of cached acorns will be consumed by the squirrel that cached them or by another squirrel that "pilfers" their cache. It is now suspected that the acorns that sprout from caches are not those that have been forgotten; they are the caches of squirrels that have been killed by predators. A broad-winged hawk settles in the top of a red pine above me, scattering tawny chipmunks everywhere. I smile, knowing that the hawk is as essential to the life of the oaks as any squirrel.

I work my way across the patch cut, bending and planting. For an acorn to sprout, it must have survived two years of drought and weevils and parasites on its parent tree. It must have been fortunate enough to be cached by a more mutualistically minded rodent, and then to have that rodent be killed by a predator. That any acorn survives this gauntlet is nothing short of a miracle.

For the acorns that manage this incredible feat at Bear Island, sprouting will be just the beginning. In the openness of the patch cuts, the oak seedlings will race fast-growing aspen and paper birch, stump-sprouting red maple, and beech clones connected to expansive, established root systems. They will compete against tens of thousands of trees of dozens of different species, each rushing toward the same open door. As they do, they will suffer the browsing of deer and the girdling teeth of rodents, insects and disease, drought and inundation, late frosts and early snows, an endless parade of perils that they must simply endure, rooted in place.

It should be impossible, but somehow it is not. Decades ago, the oaks in the patch cut were acorns themselves, scattered across the leaves, cached in secret places. Each of these oaks escaped the deer and the bears and the turkeys, outcompeted thousands of their peers, weathered the stressors of this changed and changing world. Now they endow the world with acorns of their own, sending their progeny on the same unlikely journey.

A squirrel bounds away, its cheeks full of acorns. Unlike the squirrel, I am gifted and burdened with choice, free to choose what my relationship with this forest will be. I can decide to heal this place or to push it further into dysfunction, to do what is necessary or to do nothing. I can decide if I will plant acorns or not, if I will be mutualistic or antagonistic, if I will be a keystone individual.

My acorn-planting stick pokes another hole in the dry soil. This year, a single oak may produce tens of thousands of acorns, an opulent display in the starving forest of the mountain. The energy hidden in these acorns could have made the oaks rich; it could have helped them grow taller and wider, could have helped them overtop their neighbors, could have helped them defend themselves from the forest's many stressors. Instead, the acorns fall from their branches and litter the ground, nourishing the bodies of squirrels and deer and turkeys.

Like the oaks, I give many extravagant and futile gifts. I spend my time and my energy casting acorns over the earth, doing so many sweet and unreasonable things, using so much of my power and my freedom to create wealth that I will never reap. Like the oaks, I must not mourn the acorns that are eaten, parasitized, or lost, must not dwell on my failures. Like the oaks, I must know that if a single acorn in fifty thousand becomes an oak that reaches the canopy, my sacrifice was not in vain. The oaks embody a defiant vision: a reimagining of what it means to live a good life, a reimagining of what it means to be wealthy, a reimagining of what it means to be truly free.

I stand to stretch my aching back. The work is everlasting; hundreds of acorns rest in the earth like tiny beating hearts, each covered by an inch of tender soil. There are thousands more still to plant. In my life I will plant many acorns, sow many seeds of beauty, nurture many impossible dreams. Again and again I will bury acorns in the earth in the hope that they will practice the ancient art of emergence, becoming a small part of a world worth saving.

Such actions will never be profitable, glamorous, or easy to explain. I will do these things not because they are easy but because they are right. I will do these things because I want to leave a better legacy, because I want to live in a world that is a little more beautiful.

I will always be rich knowing that the forests of my life are filled with acorns.

The sky is bright and blue, streaked with clouds as thin as carded wool. A cloud of red dust lingers in the air as I weave between stumps, bent like an elder. The patch cut is as still as the waters of a new beaver pond. The forest hangs limbo, a brief pause in its perpetual arc of change.

I stand and squint into the sun. To the west, the sky roils darkly. Clouds gather over *hitawbagw*—the lake between—shading the ageless cedars twisting from its limestone bluffs. As I watch, the clouds move east, crossing the paved streets of the city and entering the broad valley. Behind them, a wall of rain sweeps the earth like a wedding train.

Below the cliffs and across the highway, the big river sparkles faintly through the trees. Once the river kissed the feet of this mountain, fish teeming in its beaver ponds and in the riffles of its clear waters. Once it soared into a lake with an unbroken shoreline, undivided by concrete dams and bridges and causeways.

Once this was a forest of ancient, massive beech, their trunks marked by generations of black bears, their roots anchored in deep, dark soil. Once this was a forest traversed by eastern elk, their ears listening for the rustling of wolves. Once this was a multigenerational forest, shaped by thousands of years of death and change: by windstorms and ice storms, by passenger pigeons and beavers. Once the forest on the mountain was just a single piece of a forest that spanned horizons, a world of natural communities and human communities integrated across a boundless landscape. I can only imagine how this forest of the past would have looked and sounded and smelled, how the light would have touched it on an October day like this. Though I have never known a forest like this, somehow I miss it deeply.

As I plant another acorn, the big woods are gone from the broad valley, the river dammed and diked, the wildlife and the fish pressed to the boundaries of their lives and the limits of their resilience. The endless forest has been shattered into pieces, roads piercing its deepest and most secret hollows. The forest that remains is a legacy of colonization and genocide, ecosystems destroyed and species driven to extinction, the prosperity of some paid for in the bodies of others.

I press an acorn into an oak stump, its wood softened by time. Decades ago, this tree was cut with a chainsaw and dragged to the clearing by a roaring skidder. Decades ago, the oak's trunk was bucked into logs, loaded onto a truck, brought to the roaring mill across the mountains, sliced into red, fragrant boards. Today, that mill is abandoned, tilting and rotten, its machines rusting in the fog. The world has moved on. The mill sinks into obsolescence.

Today, the stumps and the crowns of the oaks are infused with miles of fungal thread, scored by bear claws, colonized by covens of black ants. Today, thousands of tiny creatures are hard at work turning these scaffolds of cellulose and lignin into soil that will nourish the forest of the future. Today, a community of living things are building something beautiful for whomever and whatever may follow. As the mill drifts slowly to the ground, the oaks defy erasure.

I press another acorn between the flared roots of a red maple stump, cut only weeks ago, its white wood just beginning to darken. When I first walked this mountain, I saw a forest of ghosts and shadows, a forest that was half of itself, a forest that was the memory of something beautiful, lost long ago. I have begun to build a new legacy, to reimagine this forest from the pieces and parts left to me, a vision as vibrant and as defiant as the rotting oak.

Next spring, acorns will split like melons from their pointed tips. Crimson roots will dive into the flinty soil, white shoots rising timidly into an awakening forest. Soon a whorl of oak leaves will spread between the beech and the ferns and the partridgeberry. Like me, the little oaks are revolutionaries, and their cause is life. We will not be erased.

The storm clouds stamp their feet. They are corralled along the shifting path of the big river, thundering between the walls of the broad valley. The clouds move west, driven like cattle toward the mountains.

The light turns dim and ominous, the leaves of the trees fluttering anxiously, the sounds of the forest suddenly raucous in the still air. I lean on my acorn-planting stick as dark clouds cross the sun, turning the Big Patch into something bleak and brutal and ugly. For a moment I see the patch cut as someone else might see it, how I would once have seen it: a wasteland, a monument to oppression and destruction and carelessness and greed. For a moment, I wonder: What evil person would do this to a forest? What callousness must fill their twisted heart?

Through the gloaming, I remember Vermont's young forests, grown out of so many pastures, missing so many pieces of themselves, beset by so many threats and challenges. I do not know if I can save this forest. All I know is that it is beyond inaction, that it will not save itself. The light changes, and I remember that this patch cut is an act of love, a switchback on the winding path toward a better world.

As empty as it often feels, there is something beautiful about a life lived in the aftermath. Here, in the junkyard of the Anthropocene, we hold the fate of the world—all its ecosystems, all its peoples—in our hands. In this moment, we can allow this bio-sphere, our home, to sink further into dysfunction and disarray, or we can make the radical and bittersweet decisions necessary to choose a different path. This world is like the forest that stood here a month ago, with little to lose and everything to gain. Inside of this catalyzing moment, we have the opportunity to reimagine our relationship to ecosystems and our relationship to each other: to redefine what we are and what is precious to us.

As empty as they often feel, there is something beautiful about a landscape of forests that are just a fraction of their true potential. The forests of our lives are still only at the beginning of their journeys; they may yet become diverse and complex, rich with legacies, ancient again. With our help, these forests may rediscover a capacity for life beyond imagining, an abundance that this world has not known for generations.

I pick up another acorn, another product of thousands of years of adaptation and change, another precious thing chained to the legacies of the past and hurtling toward an uncertain future. Perhaps it is doomed. Perhaps it contains endless possibilities.

Humidity cloaks the land, drawing tiny, round beads of sweat from my skin. For a moment the mountain is cast in golden light, its smells sharp and strong. As my fingers touch another acorn, a raindrop strikes the back of my hand, rolling between the small bones of my fingers. Suddenly, droplets are stippling the soil like falling stars, throwing up little clouds of dust. I have nowhere to be and so I kneel, watching the water run around the stumps and the upturned leaves, drawing spiderwebs on the earth.

High on the mountain, the storm shakes the brittle needles of the red pines, the scarlet crown cresting the brow of the cliffs. The rain soaks the talus where bears have slept through thousands of winters, the boulders that fill the fissures in the mountain like an ancient river. It darkens the hidden outcrop that is the profile of an old man's face, his lips slightly parted.

The storm fills the air of the plateau where I will spend a deer season watching the sun rise over Bone Mountain, catching a single glimpse of an antlered buck in the blowing snow. It coats the bark of the Sentinel Oak, its gnarled branches reaching in every direction: the king of the rocks and the cliffs, an elder defying all sense of time.

The stormwaters swirl into the belly of the Big Bowl, where the high ridge of Stimson Mountain bends like the body of an old woman, her hands cupped, the twin waters of Bear Island Brook and Berta Brook spilling forever through her fingers. They join the waters of the endless spring that rise through some wound in the bedrock, born into this tender place in the iron regime of the mountain, this locus where all things gather.

The storm crosses Bear Alley, where the bears teach their cubs to climb, passing over the strand of hemlock where I will someday take a small buck, its head raised toward me. It flows into Bear Island Brook, meandering over rocks and through soft, green places, licking the roots of sedges and false nettle. It descends deer trails and skid trails, channels down branches and trunks, permeates the winking pores of the orange soil and rolls over the bedrock below. It passes through life and death, through legacies I inherited and through legacies I will leave for future generations.

Someday, I will tell my children that the caves in the talus are a womb, the origin of all the black bears on the mountain, and that the Big Bowl is the source of all its waters. Someday, I will walk these trails with my children and teach them to reimagine forests as communities of complexity and depth and expansiveness: communities that are fated to change, to celebrate both the miracle of life and the miracle of death. Someday, I will kneel beside these stumps, a young forest blooming around me, and teach my children the imperfect truth of what it means to love a forest.

Someday, I will teach my children that this world is not ours to hold but that we hold it anyway, that each of us is a steward for one brief and precious moment in time. In our short lives, we must learn to pair power and freedom with humility, to embody responsibility and relationship, even when it breaks our hearts. A better world will be built by our hands and our choices, strengthened by trauma and by loss, by failure and resilience, by joy and beauty, by the inefficiencies of kindness. Someday, I will teach my children that, despite everything, we are destined to thrive—that we are destined to live in a world that is beautiful.

In the years to come, the traces of this moment will fade. This empty patch cut will have become a diverse young forest, the stumps softening and mixing with those of the oaks cut decades ago. I will walk through this young forest and remember this autumn day, when my hands were young. I will remember that each tall, perfect oak was once an acorn between my fingertips, that this forest is a child of responsibility—something that we could only have embodied together. No one but me will ever truly know the pieces of myself that I have left on this mountain, the labor of love that being the steward of this land has been. I will know, and that is enough.

We owe too much to the future to be imprisoned by the past. As the storm passes over me, I am grateful to be anything at all, grateful to be alive at a time when there is so much worth saving. I want to live in the world that will arise from this moment, the world built by people who are brave and humble and resilient, who make countless bittersweet compromises, who live their lives with the dream of a better world burning in their chests. I want to live in a world that will be created by people planting acorns in the rain.

The waters of the storm flow around me, rolling through patch cuts like kettles of silver fog. They flow through the clearing, where a wheelbarrow of stones rests forgotten in the mud. They touch the roots of the Memory Tree, a tree that will someday be a giant.

A decade ago, a young man went blind in one eye. Broken and battered as he was, he found his way to this mountain, this island, this leaking ship keeling on the seas of change. Imperfect as he was, he summoned what little courage he had and decided to make this place shine again, day by flickering day.

I feel that young man inside me as I plant an acorn, as the teeth of my chainsaw spin, as a deer steps into my crosshairs, as I draw a thin mist of herbicide across another barberry, as I engage in the many sacred and bittersweet acts of healing this world.

Sometimes this life feels like autumn: the exhausted end of a boundless summer. Today I choose to live in a world in which spring is just breaking, impossible and inevitable—a world that is just awakening, just beginning to discover what it truly is. I look toward the broken ridge of the mountain and feel a powerful nostalgia, not for the past but for the future. High above the storm, the light is swelling, calling everything upward, toward a world that is just beginning. I am trying.

I bend and plant another acorn.

AFTERWORD

Each morning, the man awoke at dawn in his little wooden house, filling his clay mug with coffee from a distant forest. Each morning he wrote a little more in a book that seemed like it would never be finished, each morning pressing it a little farther forward. Each morning he struggled against hopelessness, against the weight of a task that seemed endless and impossible. Somehow, he persisted, moving toward the future with the steadfastness and the resilience of a forest.

As he wrote, the phoebes perched on their nests in the eaves. The rain fell outside his window, tapping on the glass. Across the mountain, the raindrops coated the leaves of the trees, trickled from twig to branch, rushed through the cracks in their bark and into the waiting soil. As it always had, the water ran downhill, gathering in the mountain's rocky streams, flowing into the big river. Everything was the same as it ever was, and everything was changed forever.

Five years ago, I began writing this book. For five years I woke before dawn each morning and typed for an hour before heading into the woods. It was a simple and futile act, more of a practice than a task that could ever be completed. Now, somehow, I have finished, my message in a bottle cast indelicately into the surf. The waters are cold and endless, touching every shore. I wonder what it means to finish something in a world without endings.

Since beginning this journey, the world has changed forever. As I wrote, the planet staggered through a global pandemic, wars spread, people were killed and displaced by climate change, species were driven to extinction, tens of thousands of acres of forest were lost in my home state of Vermont alone. As this book grew and changed, I suffered and healed from a debilitating injury, traded my old tractor for a skidder, planted dozens of orchard trees, sprayed gallons of herbicide, cut hundreds of cords of firewood and tens of thousands of board feet of timber. As I wrote, the seedlings in the patch cuts on the mountain reached over my head, becoming thickets too dense to cross. As I shaped these chapters, one hour at a time, the clearing was transformed from a barren desert to a meadow of wildflowers; this morning, monarch butterflies are drifting through the milkweed and the elderberry bushes are heavy with purple fruit. As this book neared completion, I conserved Bear Island, protecting the forest on the mountain forever.

Two years ago, I walked through another high-graded and unhealthy stand of trees, another tangle of rutted skid trails bleeding murky water down the hill. I kicked at the rotting stumps, swearing, as I had years before, that there were no healthy trees there—that there was nothing worth saving. And yet, this was Bear Island. My roots had sunk deep into these rocks, my relationship and responsibility toward this land becoming something that no adversity could destroy. I could not do nothing.

Today, my little house stands at the bottom of that hill. Each morning, as the light touches the mountains, I look through its windows and into a forest that I once called hopeless. Two years ago, as I cut countless unhealthy trees—another declining ash, another fading paper birch, another stunted red maple, another diseased beech—I found that a healthy forest was there after all, waiting to be unearthed. This morning sugar maples, yellow birches, and red oaks stand proudly on the hillside, their branches full, their trunks tall and beautiful. The forest around them is a beautiful mess: its canopy blessed by gaps of different shapes and sizes, its floor a tangle of trunks and treetops. Aspens lean, waiting for pileated woodpeckers to fill them with holes, and legacy trees stand among the young, serving no other purpose than to exist. Morning after morning I stand at the window of my little house, on floors of ash and paper birch and red maple, the woodstove glowing with cords of split beech, and watch the forest on the hillside with pride and hope.

A beautiful forest grows on the hillside of this world. It is a forest of justice and equity, biodiversity and ecological integrity, a world that honors both the intrinsic value of this biosphere and the intrinsic value of its people. Like the oaks and the sugar maples on the hillside, the pieces of this forest are already here, waiting to be discovered. This forest will not be unearthed through inaction or subjugation, through stubbornness or complacency—only through relationship and responsibility, humility and courage, pragmatism and change. We already have the power to make this forest a reality—we just need to choose to do so.

To love a forest is not enough. As we tend to our small and complex lives, we cannot be distracted from the fact that this world's forests, its creatures, its people will not be saved by individual action alone. Massive, institutional change—a revolution in the way that we care for and value ecosystems and the way that we care for and value each other—is needed. Without fundamental changes to this world's laws and institutions, its economic systems, without a fair and just and representative political system, without holding those with power to account, our work will ultimately be futile.

At Bear Island, the forest on the mountain lives a life without beginnings or endings. Like this world, this forest will always be a mess, always incomplete, always a map of scars. There is nowhere to arrive, no final destination to attain, no endings and no perfect solutions. There is only life: strange and imperfect, crooked and precious. This world, like this forest, like ourselves, will always be a work in progress, something that we can only embody together. That is what will make it strong. That is what will make it beautiful.

As my little house loses its shine, as I wear paths on the floorboards, the forest on the mountain will change. It will be built of ancient things and new things, human things and wild things, many things at once. As the forest and I lean on each other, as I lay my hands upon it again and again, we will embody a reimagining of what it means to love a forest, a reimagining of what it means to live in this world with compassion.

After five years, I still do not know who these words will reach or what purpose they will serve any more than I know how many of the acorns that I have planted will someday become oaks. All I can do is to plant these seeds on the rocky shoulders of the mountain, to hope against hope that I have left some mark of beauty on this precious world. On this morning, that is enough.

We reach toward a better world together. I am proud to inhabit this imperfect moment, and I am proud to share it with you, whoever you are.

Here we are. What will we do next?

NOTES

CHAPTER 1

For two millennia: Elizabeth H. Thompson, Eric R. Sorenson, and Robert J. Zaino, *Wetland, Woodland, Wildland: A Guide to the Natural Communities of Vermont* (White River Junction, VT: Chelsea Green Publishing, 2019).

Research suggests that this bias: Edward O. Wilson, *The Future of Life* (New York: Knopf Doubleday Publishing Group, 2003).

They would see the old-growth forest: Mary Byrd Davis, ed., *Eastern Old Growth Forests: Prospects for Rediscovery and Recovery* (Washington, DC: Island Press, 1996); Andrew M. Barton and William S. Keeton, *Ecology and Recovery of Eastern Old Growth Forests* (Washington, DC: Island Press, 2018); and Jon R. Luoma, *The Hidden Forest: The Biography of an Ecosystem* (New York: Henry Holt, 1999).

Embedded within scientific forestry: Brian J. Palik, Anthony W. D'Amato, Jerry F. Franklin, and Norman K. Johnson, *Ecological Silviculture: Foundations and Applications* (Long Grove, IL: Waveband Press, Inc., 2021).

As people have learned more about: For an example of anthropomorphizing and mythologizing, see Peter Wohlleben, *The Hidden Life of Trees: What They Feel, How They Communicate* (Berkely, CA: Greystone Books, 2015).

A recent analysis of the research: Justine Karst, Melanie D. Jones, and Jason D. Hoeksema, "Positive Citation Bias and Overinterpreted Results Lead to Misinformation on Common

Mycorrhizal Networks in Forests," *Nature Ecology and Evolution* 7 (February 13, 2023): 501–11, https://doi.org/10.1038/s41559 -023-01986-1.

CHAPTER 2

To the south: Rich Holschuh, "Mountain Names: Remembering Their Aboriginal Origins," *Green Mountain Club*, October 17, 2019, https://tinyurl.com/ztprzxdx.

Two hundred and fifty years ago: Thomas G. Siccama, "Presettlement and Present Forest Vegetation in Northern Vermont with Special Reference to Chittenden County," *The American Midland Naturalist* 85, no. 1 (1971): 153–72.

Across this continent: Charles C. Mann, *1491: New Revelations of the Americas before Columbus* (New York: Knopf, 2005); Alice Outwater, *Water: A Natural History* (New York: Basic Books, 1996); and Eric Rutkow, *American Canopy: Trees, Forests and the Making of a Nation* (New York: Scribner, 2012).

By the mid-1800s: Rutkow, *American Canopy.*

By 1850: Vermont Historical Society, "Sheep in Vermont," *Vermont History Explorer*, accessed February 10, 2023, https://tinyurl.com/23n245xe; Tom Wessels, *Reading the Forested Landscape: A Natural History of New England* (Woodstock, VT: The Countryman Press, 1997).

While forests now cover: "Vermont Forests 2017," USDA Forest Service, Resource Bulletin NRS-120, 2020, fpr.vermont.gov.

The 1800s marked a moment: Ben Goldfarb, *Eager: The Surprising, Secret Life of Beavers and Why They Matter* (White River Junction, VT: Chelsea Green Publishing, 2018).

Across the eighteenth: Tom Rogers, "History Space: Vermont's Great Outdoors," Burlington Free Press, accessed February 10, 2023, https://tinyurl.com/y7w7p594.

The herds of hundreds of millions: Philip Lee, *Restigouche: The Long Run of the Wild River* (Fredericton, NB: Goose Lane Editions, 2020); Outwater, *Water.*

Some wildlife species: Rogers, "History Space."

As I kneel on the hillside: "Living Planet Report 2022," World Wildlife Fund, October 1, 2022, https://tinyurl.com/mp2nfk28.

One million others: IPBES (2019): E. S. Brondizio, J. Settele, S. Díaz, and H. T. Ngo, eds., "Global Assessment Report on Biodiversity and Ecosystem Services of the Intergovernmental Science-Policy Platform on Biodiversity and Ecosystem Services," IPBES secretariat, Bonn, Germany, 1148 pages, https://doi.org/10.5281/zenodo.3831673 (link is external); United Nations, "UN Report: Nature's Dangerous Decline 'Unprecedented'; Species Extinction Rates 'Accelerating'—United Nations Sustainable Development," United Nations Sustainable Development, May 6, 2019, https://tinyurl.com/mrskjhta.

CHAPTER 3

The creatures with which they shared: Rogers, "History Space."

Soon, a pair of ornate leaves: Western Abnaki-English Dictionary | Glosbe, *Glosbe.com*, accessed February 10, 2023, glosbe.com/abe/en/senomoziak.

Then a pair of delicate leaves: Western Abnaki-English Dictionary | Glosbe, *Glosbe.com*, accessed February 10, 2023, glosbe.com/abe/en/anaskemezi.

CHAPTER 4

Besides providing unique habitat: Goldfarb, *Eager.*

By the 1800s: "Beaver Wars, Summary, Facts, Significance, Timeline, Colonial America," American History Central, https://tinyurl.com/2x5ezcj8; Goldfarb, *Eager;* Outwater, *Water.*

Four hundred years ago: Outwater, *Water.*

Historical accounts describe these flocks: John James Audubon, *The Birds of America: From Drawings Made in the United States and Their Territories* (New York: J.J. Audubon and J.B. Chevalier, 1944); David

Biello, "3 Billion to Zero: What Happened to the Passenger Pigeon?," *Scientific American*, June 27, 2014, https://tinyurl.com/49jzbknd.

One of these curious roosting-places: Audubon, *Birds of America*, plate 62.

Early successional forests are underrepresented: M. Lapin, "Old-Growth Forests: A Literature Review of the Characteristics of Eastern North American Forests" (Montpelier: Vermont Natural Resources Council, 2005); Eric Sorenson and Robert Zaino, "Vermont Conservation Design: Maintaining and Enhancing an Ecologically-Functional Landscape. Summary Report for Landscapes, Natural Communities, Habitats, and Species" (Montpelier: Vermont Agency of Natural Resources, 2018).

Many of the species that depend on them are in decline: "The Status of Vermont Forest Birds: A Quarter Century of Monitoring" (White River Junction: Vermont Center for Ecostudies, 2017).

Tree cavities provide nesting: Richard M. DeGraaf and Alex L. Shigo, "Managing Cavity Trees for Wildlife in the Northeast," *General Technical Reports* NE-101 (Broomall, PA: US Department of Agriculture, Forest Service, Northeastern Forest Experimental Station, 1985), 22.

In a world in which a dead tree: Jon R. Luoma, *The Hidden Forest: The Biography of an Ecosystem* (New York: Henry Holt, 1999).

Slowly, its essence will be dissolved: "Vermont Forests 2017" (2020). USDA Forest Service. Resource Bulletin NRS-120.

CHAPTER 5

Thirteen thousand years ago: Thompson et al., *Wetland, Woodland, Wildland*.

a steppe roamed by wooly mammoths: David J. Meltzer, "Overkill, Glacial History, and the Extinction of North America's Ice Age Megafauna," *Proceedings of the National Academy of Sciences* 117 (2020): 28555–63.

Ten thousand years ago: Michael Balter, "What Killed the Great Beasts of North America?," *Science*, January 28, 2014, https://tinyurl.com/345d8hhr.

Where the neighborhood now stands: Thompson et al., *Wetland, Woodland, Wildland.*

Stacks of pine boards: "History of Forestry in Vermont | Department of Forests, Parks and Recreation," Vermont.gov, 2021, https://tinyurl.com/4m98pcfp.

The opulence of the 1800s: George Perkins Marsh, *Man and Nature; or Physical Geography as Modified by Human Action* (New York: Charles Scribner, 1865).

In the 1950s: Mark Bushnell, "Then Again: Bulk Milk Tanks Altered the Family Farm Way of Life," VTDigger, January 13, 2019, https://tinyurl.com/4n96zd8b.

None is a means: Brian J. Palik et al., *Ecological Silviculture: Foundations and Applications* (Long Grove, IL: Waveband Press, Inc., 2021).

"Every corpse is an ecosystem": Edward O. Wilson, *Tales from the Ant World* (New York: Liverright Publishing Corporation, 2021).

CHAPTER 6

The highway turns and tracks south: Kevin Dann, "Vermont's Original Forest Language," *Vermont Woodlands* (Winter 1994): 14–16.

For this reason, some researchers and botanists: B. Oborny, "The Plant Body as a Network of Semi-autonomous Agents: A Review," *Philosophical Transactions of the Royal Society B Biological Sciences* 374, no. 1774 (June 10, 2019): 20180371, https://doi.org/10.1098/rstb.2018.0371; PMID: 31006361; PMCID: PMC6553591; D. G. Sprugel, T. M. Hinckley, and W. Schaap, "The Theory and Practice of Branch Autonomy," *Annual Review of Ecology and Systematics* 22 (1991): 309–34.

The sun rises over Moziozagan: Holschuh, "Mountain Names."

CHAPTER 7

As forests blur: Elizabeth Kolbert, *The Sixth Extinction: An Unnatural History* (New York: Picador, 2014); Edward O. Wilson,

Half-Earth: Our Planet's Fight for Life (New York: Liveright Publishing Corporation, 2016).

Within this living system: Suzanne Simard and Daniel Durall, "Mycorrhizal Networks: A Review of Their Extent, Function, and Importance," *Canadian Journal of Botany* 82, no. 8 (August 2004): 1140–1165.

At least one-third of the species: Wilson, *The Diversity of Life.* Edward O. Wilson, *The Diversity of Life* (Cambridge, MA: Belknap Press, 1992).

Three centuries ago: Rogers, "History Space."

I thought that fewer wolves: Aldo Leopold, *A Sand County Almanac* (New York: Oxford University Press, 1949), 130–32.

Like a chosen few: Rogers, "History Space."

At a time when forests' best hope: A. W. D'Amato, P. C. Catanzaro, and E. S. Huff, *Increasing Forest Resiliency for an Uncertain Future,* Cooperative Extension Landowner Outreach Pamphlet (Boston, 2016).

The earth shudders: Kolbert, *The Sixth Extinction.*

CHAPTER 8

In every handful of forest soil: Luoma, *The Hidden Forest.*

Tiny creatures moved: Robin Wall Kimmerer, *Braiding Sweetgrass: Indigenous Wisdom, Scientific Knowledge, and the Teachings of Plants* (Minneapolis: Milkweed Editions, 2013).

Of the ten million: Wilson, *Half-Earth.*

About 90 percent of the cells: F. E. Dewhirst et al., "The Human Oral Microbiome," *Journal of Bacteriology* 192, no. 19 (October 2020): 5002–17.

Our skin is like the bark: Michael Eisenstein, "The Skin Microbiome," *Nature* 588, no. 7838 (December 16, 2020): S209; E. A. Grice and J. A. Segre, "The Skin Microbiome," *Nature Reviews Microbiology* 9, no. 4 (April 2011): 244–53, https://doi.org/10.1038/nrmicro 2537. Erratum in *Nature Reviews Microbiology* 9, no. 8 (August 2011): 626, PMID: 21407241; PMCID: PMC3535073.

If I wished, I could fight: Mary M. Berlik et al., "The Illusion of Preservation: A Global Environmental Argument for the Local Production of Natural Resources," *Journal of Biogeography* 29 (2002): 1557–68.

The growing body of research: Robert J. Brulle and David N. Pellow, "Environmental Justice: Human Health and Environmental Inequalities," *Annual Review of Public Health* 27, no. 1 (2006): 103–24; Robert D. Bullard et al., "Toxic Wastes and Race at Twenty 1987–2007: A Report Prepared for the United Church of Christ Justice & Witness Ministries" (Cleveland, OH: United Church of Christ, 2007); Benjamin F. Chavis, "Toxic Waste and Race in the United States" (Cleveland, OH: United Church of Christ, 1987); P. Mohai and R. Saha, "Which Came First, People or Pollution? A Review of Theory and Evidence from Longitudinal Environmental Justice Studies," *Environmental Research Letters* 10, no. 12 (2015): 125011, https://doi.org/10.1088/1748-9326/10/12/125011.

Your job is to find out: William Stafford, *The Way It Is: New and Selected Poems* (St. Paul: Graywolf Press, 1998).

CHAPTER 9

Biodiversity: Wilson, *Half-Earth*; Wilson, *The Future of Life*.

At least 680 vertebrate species: WWF, "Living Planet Report 2022"; United Nations, "UN Report: Nature's Dangerous Decline 'Unprecedented.'"

According to the National Wildlife Federation: "Invasive Species," National Wildlife Federation, accessed January 2, 2024, https://tinyurl.com/2kvtrmcc.

Globally, the major threats: Wilson, *Half-Earth*.

Across oceans: I. Soto et al., "Global Economic Costs of Herpetofauna Invasions," *Scientific Reports* 12 (2022): 10829, https://doi.org/10.1038/s41598-022-15079-9; Małgorzata Stanek et al., "Invasive Red Oak (Quercus Rubra L.) Modifies Soil Physicochemical Properties and Forest Understory Vegetation," *Forest Ecology and Management*

472 (September 2020): 118253, https://doi.org/10.1016/j.foreco
.2020.118253; "Why North America Black Cherry Tree Is
Invasive in Europe," *ScienceDaily*, July 28, 2009, https://tinyurl.com
/hwkwbdjf; Laura Bonesi and Santiago Palazon, "The American
Mink in Europe: Status, Impacts, and Control," *Biological Conservation*
134, no. 4 (February 2007): 470–83, https://doi.org/10.1016/j.biocon
.2006.09.006.

As invasive plants spread: Liam Heneghan et al., "The Invasive
Shrub European Buckthorn (Rhamnus Cathartica, L.) Alters Soil
Properties in Midwestern US Woodlands," *Applied Soil Ecology* 32
(2006): 142–48, https://doi.org/10.1016/j.apsoil.2005.03.009;
M. E. Rout and R. M. Callaway, "Interactions between Exotic
Invasive Plants and Soil Microbes in the Rhizosphere Suggest
That 'Everything Is Not Everywhere,'" *Annals of Botany* 110, no.
2 (2012): 213–22, https://doi.org/10.1093/aob/mcs061; PMID:
22451600; PMCID: PMC3394644.

CHAPTER 10

The populations of these animals: Jerry O. Wolff, "Population
Fluctuations of Mast-Eating Rodents Are Correlated with
Production of Acorns," *Journal of Mammalogy* 77, no. 3 (1996):
850–56, https://doi.org/10.2307/1382690.

Of the acorns: Jimmy Galford et al., "Insects Affecting Establishment
of Northern Red Oak Seedlings in Central Pennsylvania," in
*Proceedings of the 8th Central Hardwood Forest Conference, University Park,
Pennsylvania, March 4–6, 1991,* ed. Larry H. McCormick and Kurt
W. Gottschalk, General Technical Reports NE-148 (Radnor, PA:
Northeastern Forest Experiment Station, 1991), 271–80; David L.
Loftis and Charles E. McGee, eds., "Oak Regeneration: Serious
Problems Practical Recommendations (Symposium Proceedings),"
General Technical Reports SE-84 (Asheville, NC: U.S. Department
of Agriculture, Forest Service, Southeastern Forest Experiment
Station, 1993), 319; D. A. Marquis, P. L. Ekert, and B. A. Roach,

"Acorn Weevils, Rodents, and Deer All Contribute to Oak Regeneration Difficulties in Pennsylvania," Res. Pap. NE-356 (Upper Darby, PA: US Department of Agriculture, Forest Service, Northeastern Forest Experiment Station, 1976).

In an acorn year: Loftis and McGee, "Oak Regeneration," 319.

Some individuals are more antagonistic: A. M. Brehm, "Small Mammal Personalities Generate Context Dependence in the Seed Dispersal Mutualism," *Proceedings of the National Academy of Sciences of the United States of America* 119, no. 15 (April 2022): e2113870119, https://doi.org/10.1073/pnas.2113870119; PMID: 35377818; PMCID: PMC9169644.

It is now suspected: Michael A. Steele, *Oak Seed Dispersal: A Study in Plant-Animal Interactions* (Baltimore: Johns Hopkins University Press, 2021).